A Better Way

Ethical Wisdom from the Ancient Sages

Edited by
Partap Singh

ALIGHT BOOKS, SAN FRANCISCO

A BETTER WAY
An Alight Book

Visit our website at
www.alightbooks.com

PRINTING HISTORY
Alight edition / December 2010

Cover and text design © 2010 by Partap Singh

For information address: Alight Publications
a division of Alight Natural Products Limited
P.O. Box 930, Union City, California 94587.
www.alightbooks.com

ISBN: 1-931833-35-6

ALIGHT
Alight Books are published by Alight Publications
a division of Alight Natural Products Limited
P.O. Box 930, Union City, California 94587.

PRINTED IN THE UNITED STATES OF AMERICA

Contents

Introduction	5
Advice to the King - The Testament of Morann	15
The Gentleman - The Analects of Confucius	21
The Emperor - The Meditations of Marcus Aurelius	41
The Prince - The Dhammapada of The Buddha	79
The Prophet - The Teachings of Jesus Christ	121
The Spiritual Man - The Yoga Sutras of Patanjali	139
Conclusion	155

Introduction

The modern is often depicted as fast-paced, fluid, and ever-changing. It is contrasted with a frighteningly static picture of traditional life. But what has really sped up to give us this sense of modernity? Certainly not the pace with which we think or our mental capacity, since evolution occurs on far larger timescales, and even a cursory study of ancient philosophy will prove deep insight existed thousands of years ago. Only the volume and velocity of information flow has really been increased, and this alone can explain all the phenomena we associate with the modern world.

We have access to ever more information at ever increasing speeds, but the same old brains with which to process all of it. More troubling is the fact that our brains are somehow producing all of this, and there is the distinct impression that we are favoring quantity over quality of thought. In a time, not so long ago, when it took substantial effort to get a work penned, or in print, the thoughts recorded for the world to see would be carefully considered. Even in the days of the typewriter, it was a pain to make a mistake and every word would get some attention. Today, the internet, and especially the most recent incarnation of it, has convinced people that their most trivial thoughts are worth airing. The result is a morass of useless information that the earnest seeker of wisdom has to wade through in the hopes of grasping a nugget worth the time and effort.

The lack of time is a major reason for the stress we often feel. After all, the duration of our lives has not kept pace with this boom in information, either. The tech-savvy are those best able to keep up with it all, and they do so through filtering techniques that focus their minds on the important ideas – at least, the ideas that they have been conditioned to think are important. People have also learned to keep their statements short, because otherwise they don't have the time to contact others as frequently as is now expected. But in this we can also see what we have lost – depth and introspection. With our time increasingly occupied by absorbing input from outside, we find quiet reflection to be novel or uncomfortable. This can be contrasted with the experience of the pre-modern worker, who had ample time but lacked the knowledge base we have access to. We have access to knowledge, but don't have the time thanks to stress-inducing clutter. Eventually, perhaps we will stabilize at some happy equilibrium – a middle ground on which we will have both access and time to appreciate it.

Another side-effect of this phase of the communication revolution is a desperate need for ethics and morality. I do not believe that the modern world is in any way less moral or ethical than previous forms of society in human history. In fact, it is necessarily better. You see, ethics and morality are the cornerstones of human interaction – they mediate what we can and cannot do and say to each other. The greater ease of interaction demands a greater grasp of those fundamentals. Fortunately, most of the code is innate and a component of our evolution as social creatures. The rest, though, is bound up in culture, and in the era of loud voices all seeking attention, conflicting cultural standards are difficult to resolve. They also crop up with ever increasing speed as it is easier for different cultures to come in contact with each other. I have found that adopting a set of principles not bound up in one particular culture or another has proved valuable in guiding my conduct, and that is what I hope to present here.

This volume contains selections from the words of Confucius, Marcus Aurelius, Buddha, Christ, and Patanjali. They are organized in order of practical applicability, with Confucius the most easy to apply to daily life, and Patanjali the most difficult. These great figures explained their views succinctly, and all continue to be relevant despite the changes that have occurred over time. Together, they present a very consistent cross-cultural perspective on human conduct and the need for personal introspection.

On the Need for Ethics and Morality

But why do we need ethics and morality of this sort? Maybe our innate sense of how we should treat others is sufficient. Or perhaps, as economists have often posited, self-interest ultimately rules all, and it is most beneficial to act in self-interest regardless of ethical or moral concerns. There is something tempting about throwing off cultural imperatives and traditional authorities. It is part of a trend that began with the Enlightenment thinkers before the modern industrial era began – one that has broadened our horizons to great benefit.

The inadequacy of our innate sense of morality is most obvious from the fact that people regularly choose to seek guidance on the issues. Life throws unexpected curveballs at us, and the correct choice is rarely as obvious as we would like. The shortfall is also clear from the large number of people who deliberately take advantage of others without the most miniscule pang of conscience. Our innate sense of how to behave toward others allows us to be socially acceptable, but there are many socially adept people who do despicable things to their neighbors.

The world of economics is replete with examples of such behavior. Why have economists adopted the principle of informed self-interest in their discourse? To put it simply, it is easy to calculate with. It is difficult to base calculations on something amorphous like morality, but self-interest in the form of monetary profit is comparatively easy. This can be seen as a useful approximation, as Milton Friedman described it to be. The problem arises when economists come to believe that this is an accurate description of reality, which is about as foolish as a physicist believing that a vacuum approximation is perfectly applicable in Earth's atmosphere and deciding to neglect air resistance. In studies examining whether people actually behave in accordance with informed self-interest, the consistent result is that the vast majority of people do not, and incorporate a greater or lesser degree of selfless action. The individuals who most conformed to self-interested behavior were, unsurprisingly, economists and stock market traders.

Is there a way to develop a scientific basis for morality instead of relying on philosophers and spiritual leaders? Well, there is certainly a rationale for ethical and moral behavior to be found in science. Biologist Richard Dawkins, in his own attempt to answer this question, pointed out that there is a direct correlation between selfless behavior and genetic similarity. In other words, we are most considerate when dealing with our family, slightly less when dealing with those of a similar background, less when dealing with humanity as a whole, less when dealing with other mammals, and least when dealing with the other creatures inhabiting the world. It is easily to mount a campaign to save the whales than to save the plankton, even though plankton is more essential to the food chain. Dawkins argues that we act in this way because it serves to perpetuate our genes. After all, the members of the human species are better than 99% genetically similar. Even if we don't have a child of our own, saving a neighbor's child gives us 99% of the benefit as far as natural selection is concerned. This is a very clever explanation for why we see ethical and moral behavior as so important, but it is not prescriptive. In other words, science does not yet have an answer about what the appropriate behaviors should be. So we have a situation in which the establishment of principled behavior is desired, informed self-interest is a theoretical approximation rather than a description of reality, and science can provide the reason for having conscientious behavior, but cannot describe what it looks like in detail. We all have an instinct for what it looks like, but without straightforward guidance to tap into, we can quickly go astray in the tumult of daily interactions. All that said, as much as we need to be concerned about our own behavior, we also need to look at the behavior of those we give power to.

In the United States, we live in a democratic system in which we get to choose our leaders. Unfortunately, we rarely seem to hold those leaders accountable for their action and attitudes. Both our political and economic leadership show a complete lack of responsibility and competence because no imperatives are placed on those with power. Since the old dictum of great power demanding great responsibility is broken at the top, regular individuals feel justified in denying their responsibility throughout the society. The damage we are doing to the environment is a poignant case, but people are only concerned about doing anything about it when its effects are at their door. When did most of the American population begin to realize the need to move away from gasoline-guzzling SUVs? When the cost of fuel reached four dollars a gallon.

Individually, we have more power than those before us could have imagined having. We have a vote, which much of the world still lacks. We have the ability to communicate our ideas as never before. In two days, we can reach any part of the populated world. Economic security in the industrialized world is at a level unimagined just a hundred years ago. Drought does not imply starvation. Our power to consume is far in excess of our actual needs. So, why don't we use such ample resources to create a better world for ourselves and for others? I believe it is simply short-sightedness. That is in turn partly due to the amount of useless or inaccurate information preventing us from relieving our ignorance on the issues and getting informed. Mainly, though, we lack guidance on the actions that would most help the situation. We lack an outline of what we should expect from ourselves and from others.

A Treatment for the Modern Reader

In this work, I have adopted a "back to basics" approach. I would like to introduce a modern audience to some of the ancient thinkers they have heard about, but haven't had the time to read. In particular, this work focuses on those who commented on how we should conduct ourselves and treat others. There are certain authorities who are broadly respected across the spectrum because they are seen as originals – they have had such immense influence over time that they are worth reading simply on that basis. Their words have been subsequently mangled and misinterpreted by so many well-meaning or opportunistic individuals that it is also a good idea to return to the source instead of picking up a later commentary or interpretation.

There are two main obstacles that may prevent a modern reader from choosing to tackle these texts. First, the spiritual or logical ideas that surround the ethical and moral precepts may seem alien. If a person is strong in their own faith, they may decide to focus on understanding the texts of that belief system more deeply instead of pursuing potentially conflicting sources outside of it. It is also possible that, knowing Aristotle's logic led him to incorrect conclusions in other matters, a person might reject him as credible. To deal with the former case, I have focused the selections on the subject at hand – how human beings should treat each other and conduct their lives – and have set all material concerning how humans should behave toward a god or

INTRODUCTION

the gods aside. The point concerning logic was resolved by the choice of authorities. Plato, Aristotle, or others who constructed logical arguments to support their statements are not included because those arguments are often so involved that they must be included in their entirety or not at all. They could be incorporated with minimal effort, but my treatment would add little to volumes that are already available.

The other obstacle is the antiquated or dense language used in typical renditions of the works. In the age of text-messaging, it can sometimes be hard to readjust to academic writing. In reworking the various translations used, I have tried to modernize and simplify the tone of the language without losing the meaning of the words. This is, of course, a tricky business, and those who spend their lives on these texts will be sure to find fault with my choices. The goal of this book is not scholarly, though, but functional. It is meant to be used practically rather than be tapped for future papers. In some cases, I have had to deal with very different wordings from two or more scholarly translations. Confronted with that problem, I either chose the more reputable translator, or constructed a middle ground that satisfied both.

Another method used to make the texts more accessible is the formatting of everything into constant verse, which is both less daunting than prose and easier to remember. In formatting the texts this way, no liberties were taken with meaning. The only point at which I hesitated in employing this tactic was with Christ's Sermon on the Mount, which is so familiar to English-speaking readers that forcing it into the constant-syllable lines will be jarring in terms of style and expectations. Otherwise, I think the format adds rather than detracts from previous treatments because it improves the flow. The ideas are now in bite-sized chunks designed to be individually chewed and digested. It is beneficial to think about each stanza before moving to the next.

The Texts

We begin with an excerpt from the Audacht Morainn – an Irish tract on kingship – adapted from a version edited by Fergus Kelly, which is the only translation used not available for consultation in the public domain. Kelly's edition is primarily of interest to linguists, and includes not only much more of the original text, but also the original Irish and a plethora of notes concerning differences between manuscripts. The rest of the works incorporated are derived from public domain translations, and are:

I. The Gentleman – Confucius' *Analects* translated by William Edward Soothill.
II. The Emperor – Marcus Aurelius' *Meditations* translated by George Long.
III. The Prince – The teachings of Buddha in the *Dhammapada* translated by Max Müller.
IV. The Prophet – Teachings of Christ from the King James Version of the Bible, and from the Gospel of Thomas (various translations are available on the internet).
V. The Spiritual Man – Patanjali's *Yoga Sutras* from a cross-referencing of two translations – the first by Charles Johnston, and the second by BonGiovanni.

I have used public domain translations so that, should the words contained here interest the reader, it will be easy to find the complete originals. With the exception of the *Yoga Sutras,* the translations are the most common ones in print. All of these works are excerpts except Patanjali's, which was short to begin with. Each selection begins with historical notes, key points about the selection, notes about the translations, and commentary. The texts themselves are presented uncluttered.

Concordances

The purpose of these selections is to demonstrate that a wide array of ancient cultures advocated compatible codes of conduct centered on numerous key principles, including:

1. The person who would best help the world is one who is not attached to it, and one as free as possible from desires that would complicate his or her judgment.
2. It is the height of decency and righteousness to fulfill one's duties and responsibilities.
3. It is possible to select the correct course of action through reason, so long as that reason is not clouded by desire or attachment.
4. Life is a tool we should wield wisely when it is ours, and respect and protect when it is in others.
5. A study of nature contributes to an understanding of the self, and examples from nature can clarify what the bustle of daily life might complicate.
6. It is through meditation that a person realizes his or her flaws, gets rid of attachment and desires, and tunes the mind to productive use.
7. It is ignorance, more than anything else, which breeds evil and failure.

These are only the most general principles shared, and as such, they may seem obvious. However, they are emphasized in greater detail and much more forcefully in the ancient writings. It is also true that, while many people can readily accept these tenets, few actually live their lives in accordance with them, or even try to.

Advice to the King
The Testament of Morann

This text is from a classic source on Irish kingship attributed to Morann, who was directing his words to Feradach Find Fechtnach. It is commonly dated to the 7th century A.D., but some linguistic features suggest an earlier date. In any case, it is the most recently composed text included here. It has a very definite rhythm built in, and is a minor marvel of rhetoric. The examples and references used in it are dated, but only a little bit of imagination is necessary to update them.

It is an excellent treatise on how power comes with certain responsibilities, and absolute power with absolute responsibility. It was directed at a medieval king who held sole sovereignty over his land. Today, we each have a piece of collective sovereignty – of the power to change the nation's policies. Does this absolve or shield us from the responsibility? Ideally, the effects of our choices would be evenly distributed throughout the nation, so we would all reap what we sow equitably. The reality is that the majority can make choices that place an unreasonable burden on the minority, and expects to face no retribution for those choices.

In the days of the medieval kings, any minority would be able to mount a threatening rebellion against a king, the recourse today is through the court system, which can test new laws against established rights. The court, rather than the king, dispenses the justice so emphasized by Morann. In the United States, Supreme Court decisions through the twentieth century served to resolve the most significant grievances of minority groups.

It is interesting to look at this tract and to ask whether those we have given power to would be as conscientious as an Irish king was advised to be. We should also ask whether, when we make decisions that will affect others, we base them on our own personal good, or on mutual benefit.

The Testament of Morann
(excerpt)

Anyone who wishes to rule wisely
Let him keep the advice which here proceeds

He who preserves justice, justice preserves
He who raises justices, justice raises
He who admires mercy, mercy admires
He who cares for his men and his people
Is cared for by his men and his people.
Let him help his men, and they will help him.
Let him soothe his men, and they will soothe him.

It is by the justice of the ruler
That plagues and storms are kept from his people.
It is by the justice of the ruler
That peace, happiness, and ease, are secured.
It is by the justice of the ruler
That each heir receives fair inheritance.
It is by the justice of the ruler
That the milk yields of cattle are maintained.
It is by the justice of the ruler
That there is an abundance of tall corn.
It is by the justice of the ruler
That the streams are replete with swimming fish.
It is by the justice of the ruler
That the young survive to succeed the old.

The young ruler should, since his rule is young
Observe the driver of a chariot
For that chariot driver does not sleep

He looks ahead, looks behind and in front
He glances to the right and to the left
He is protective to keep from breaking
With carelessness, with violence, or with haste
The wheel-rims which are running under him.

It is by the justice of the ruler
That philosophers and great men of art
Are able to grasp the crown of knowledge
And to sit and to teach the good ruling
To which he and his kin was submitted.

It is by the justice of the ruler
That the lands of each true lord so extends
Such that each cow reaches its grazing's end.

Let the ruler not resort to the red
For bloodshed destroys all attempts at rule.
Let him reciprocate any service
Let him enforce any bond he should bind
Let him do battle with breakers of oaths
Let no gifts or rich treasures or profits
Blind him to the sufferings of the weak.

Let him judge all things as they are valued
Let him estimate the earth by its fruits
Let him esteem cattle by their milk-yield
Let him judge copper by firmness and strength
Let him estimate all corn by its height
Let him esteem streams for their cleanliness
Let him judge iron by use in disputes
Let him estimate soil by production
Let him esteem sheep for their covering
Let him judge worked gold by its ornaments
Let him estimate servants by food-rent

Let him esteem craftsmen by their objects
Let him judge war bands by the lord they serve

Remember always all manners of ill
Will yield to the better and the nobler
Darkness yields to light, sorrow yields to joy
Oafs yield to sages, fools yield to wise men
Serfs yield to free men, conflict yields to peace
And meanness yields to liberality
Impetuousness yields to composure
A usurper will yield to a true lord
And above all else, falsehood yields to truth.

Let the ruler be just, merciful, firm,
Impartial, conscientious, generous,
Hospitable, honorable, stable,
Benevolent, capable, well-spoken,
Honest, steady, and in all, true-judging.

Tell him that he may die, that he will die
But how he has been, and how he will be
Is what will be proclaimed and remembered.

Here ends the advice given to the king.

The Gentleman
The Analects of Confucius

Master K'ung lived from 551 to 479 B.C. in the midst of a philosophical golden age in China. There were so many competing ideas that it is known as the Hundred Schools era, and though Confucian thought became dominant in later centuries, that was only after a long period in which it was peripheral, then persecuted. Confucius sought to educate aspiring bureaucrats in proper ethical principles. I have called him the gentleman for reasons that will be readily apparent from his words.

Confucius was a teacher and a government official during a time when China was politically fragmented. The instability meant that he spent many of his years in exile and faced more hardship than will be evident from his optimistic views about human potential. His philosophy would, after the establishment of the Han dynasty, be adopted by the ruling class and lead to a steadiness and unity scarcely imaginable in his own time.

The philosophy of Confucius is entirely focused on ethical behavior, and at its heart lies the Golden Rule (which Confucius encapsulated in the word 'reciprocity'). It is helpful to cast aside any preconceptions you might have about his philosophy, because those will almost certainly be due to later interpreters over the course of more than two thousand years. The most famous of these interpreters was Mencius, who lived two centuries after Confucius.

The Analects are a collection of quotes and notes from Confucius' students, and not his own writing. The original text often contains details about who he was speaking with when the words were recorded, but it seems as if he was prone to make random insightful comments in the natural flow of discussions. As a result, there is no rhetorical flow of the kind that can be seen in the *Dhammapada* or the words of Christ.

Chinese discourse tends to involve extensive use of references and historical examples. Even in Confucius' day, the history of what we now call China was so rich that he regularly used important figures from it as models and commented on their behavior. To avoid requiring a primer on Chinese history or frustrating footnotes, I excluded such comments. *The Analects* also include many personal comments, particularly about the philosopher's students, and these have also been left out. I have also neglected the statement "The Master said," which occurs before most of the lines of the original text.

The Analects of Confucius
(excerpts)

Is it not a pleasure to acquire
Knowledge? To exercise oneself therein?
And is it not delightful to have men
Of kindred spirit come here from afar?
For a true philosopher cherishes
No resentment, even though he, of men,
Remains unrecognized and unesteemed.

The true philosopher devotes himself
To the fundamentals. For right courses
Naturally evolve from the solid
Establishment in an unselfish life.

To conduct the government of a state
There must be religious attention to
Business and good faith, economy in
Expenditures, and love of the people.

A scholar who is not grave will inspire
No respect. He will lack stability.
He should cultivate the principles of
Conscientiousness and sincerity.
Let him have no friends unequal to him
And, when wrong, let him not wait to amend.

I will not grieve that men do not know me
I will grieve that I do not know men.

In decorum, value naturalness.
This was the admirable feature in
The regulations of the ancient kings.

And when you make a promise consistent
With what is right, then you can keep your word.
When you show respect consistent with taste,
You keep shame and disgrace at a distance.
When you have confided in one who does
Not fail his friends, you may trust him fully.

He who governs by moral excellence
May be comparable to the pole star,
As all the other stars bow towards it.

If you govern the people by the laws
And keep them in order by penalties
They may obey to avoid punishment
Yet they will surely lose their sense of shame.
Govern them by your moral excellence
And keep them in order by your conduct,
And they will still retain their sense of shame.
They will also live up to this standard.

The best type of man is not a machine.

He who keeps on reviewing old knowledge
And studies to acquire new knowledge –
He may become a teacher of others.

And concerning the nobler type of man:
He first practices what he preaches and
Then preaches according to his practice.
He is board-minded, and not prejudiced.

Learning without thinking is but useless;
Thinking without learning is dangerous.

Hear much, be reserved in what causes you
To doubt, and speak guardedly of the rest.
You will suffer little criticism.
See much, be reserved in the imprudent,
And then act guardedly as to the rest.
You will then have to bear with few regrets.

If you promote the upright and dismiss
Ill-doers, the people will be content.
If you promote ill-doers and dismiss
The upright, then there will be discontent.

To inspire, lead them with dignity,
And they will also act dutifully.
If you are kind, then they will be loyal.
Promote excellence, teach them competence
And they will each encourage the other.

To see the right, and yet not do it is
Cowardice.

In ceremonies in general, it
Is better to be simple than lavish.
In the rites of mourning, heart-felt distress
Is better than observance of detail.

Music may be readily understood
The attack should be prompt and united
The piece should proceed harmoniously
With clearness of tone, and measure of time.

A man of honor never disregards
Virtue, even during a single meal.
In the moments of haste he cleaves to it
In seasons of peril he cleaves to it.

A man's faults indicate his type of mind.
Observe his faults, and you know his virtues.

He who has heard the truth in the morning
Might die in contentment in the evening.

The student who aims at wisdom, and yet
Who is ashamed of poor clothes and poor food
Is not yet worthy to be discoursed with.

The man of honor thinks of character;
The inferior man of position.
The man of honor desires justice;
The inferior man seeks out favor.

And he who works for his own interests
Will engender much animosity.

Is a prince able to rule his country
With courtesy and with just deference?
Then what difficulty could beset him?

The wise man is informed in what is right;
The inferior man in what will pay.

When you come upon a man of great worth,
Think how you might rise up to his level.
When you come upon an unworthy man,
Then look within and examine yourself.

While a father or mother are alive
A son should not travel far. While away,
He must have a stated destination.

The age of one's parents should ever be
Kept in mind – at once for joy and for fear.

The men of old were reserved in their speech
Out of shame, lest they should come short in deed.

In serving one's prince, importunity
Results in disgrace. Importunity
Between friends results in their estrangement.

I have never yet seen a man who could
Perceive his own faults and bring the charge home.

Nature beats training – that is the rustic;
Training exceeds nature – that is the clerk.
It is only when nature and training
Are balanced – proportionately blended
That you will have the nobler type of man.

He who knows the truth is not equal to
Him who loves it, and he who loves it is
Not equal to him who delights in it.

Those who are clever delight in water
And the virtuous delight in the hills.
The clever are restless; virtuous calm.
Those who are clever can enjoy their lives
While the virtuous men prolong their lives.

How perfect is the virtue that accords
With the Golden Mean. And how rare is it.

From him who has brought his simple present
Of dried flesh, seeking to enter my school,
I have never withheld my instruction.

I expound nothing to those not earnest
Nor those not anxious to express themselves.
When I have demonstrated one angle
And he cannot bring me back the other
Three, then I do not repeat my lesson.

If wealth were a thing one could surely gain,
Even if it would mean I would have to
Become a horse's groom, I would do it.
But as one cannot count on finding it,
I will follow quests that I love better.

There are men, probably, who do things right
Without knowing at all the reason why.
I am not like that: I hear much, see much,
Select the good, follow it, treasure it.

This is the next best thing to pure knowledge.

A man cleanses himself and comes to me –
I may accept his present cleanliness
Without becoming sponsor for his past.

(In the company of someone singing,
The Master had good pieces repeated
And he joined in the melody himself.)

Courtesy uncontrolled by laws of taste
Becomes laborious effort; caution
When uncontrolled, becomes timidity;
Boldness uncontrolled becomes recklessness;
And frankness uncontrolled, effrontery.

People may be made to follow a course
But not to understand the reason why.

It is not easy to find a man who
For three years studied, yet does not seek pay.

With the impulsive yet evasive, the
Simple yet dishonest, and the stupid
Yet untruthful, I hold no acquaintance.

Am I a man who had innate knowledge?
I have no such knowledge. When a person
Uncultivated, in simplicity,
Comes to me with a question, I thrash out
Its pros and cons until I fathom it.

(Whenever the Master saw a person
In mourning, in official cap and robes,
Or one who was blind, on noticing him,
Even if the man was his own junior,
He always arose. If he was passing
Such a one, he always quickened his steps.)

I have never yet seen a man whose love
Of virtue equaled his love of woman.

The young should inspire one with respect
As their future may equal our present.
If a man has reached forty or fifty
Without being heard from, he, indeed, is
Incapable of commanding respect.

You may rob a three-corps army of its
Commander-in-chief, but still you cannot
Rob even a common man of his will.

Virtue is the denial of the self
And response to what is right and proper.
Deny yourself for one day and respond
In accord with what is right and proper,
And everyone will call you virtuous.

When abroad, act as if interviewing
An honored guest. In directing people
Act as an official in rituals.
Do not do to others what you would not
Like yourself, then your public life will not
Arouse ill-will, nor will your private life.

He who is unmoved by insidious
Soaking in of slander, or by direct
Examples of personal injury,
May truly be called a man of insight.
Indeed, he who is so unmoved by this
May also truly be called far-sighted.

Chief of the essentials of government
Are sufficient food, sufficient forces,
And the firm confidence of the people.
If you are compelled to dispense with one
Of these three, you should first forgo forces.
Compelled to eliminate another,
Choose food, for death has been the lot of all,
But a people without faith cannot stand.

I can try lawsuits as well as any,
But surely the greatest thing is to bring
About that there be no going to law.

Ponder untiringly over your plans,
Then conscientiously execute them.

The man of noble mind seeks to achieve
The good in others and not their evil.
The little-minded man is the reverse.

If you, sir, be free from the love of wealth,
Although you pay people, they will not steal.

Is there need of capital punishment?
If your aspirations are for the good,
Then, sir, the people will also be good.

The character of those in high places
Is the breeze; that of those below is grass.
With breeze upon it, the grass surely bends.

Putting duty first and success after
Will that not improve a man's character?
Attacking his own failings instead of
Others', will he not remedy his faults?

It is virtue to love your fellow men.
It is knowledge to know your fellow men.
Promote the straight and degrade the crooked
And you can make even the crooked straight.

Advise your friend conscientiously and
Guide him discreetly. If he resists it,
Then cease – do not court humiliation.

(On government, the Master said: "Be in
Advance of people, show them how to work."
Asked for more, he added: "Untiringly.")

Regarding what he does not understand,
A wise man maintains a sense of reserve.
Find correct terms. If terms be incorrect,
Then statements do not accord with the facts.
And when statements and facts do not accord,
Business is not rightly executed.
When business fails to be executed,
Order and harmony do not flourish.
When order and harmony are stifled,
Then all justice becomes arbitrary.
And when justice becomes arbitrary,

People know not how to move hand or foot.
Hence, whatever a wise man state, he can
Always define, and what he so defines,
He can always carry into practice.

Though a man may be able to recite
The three hundred Odes, when given a post,
If he proves to be without practical
Ability, or when sent anywhere,
He is unable to answer questions,
Though he knows a great deal, what use is it?

The people having grown so numerous,
What next should be done for them? – Enrich them.
When you have enriched them? – Educate them.

With good men ruling for a hundred years
The country could even tame the brutal
And abolish capital punishment.

Do not be in a hurry and do not
Be intent on minor advantages.
When one is hurried, nothing is thorough.
When one is intent on advantages
That are small, nothing great is accomplished.

In private life, you should be courteous;
Handling public business, serious.
With all men, you should be conscientious.
Even going among barbarians,
You may not relinquish these few virtues.

If I cannot obtain men to teach who
Are of the Golden Mean, of those I find,
Let them be the ambitious and discreet.
The ambitious make progress and take hold.
And concerning those who are discreet, there
Are things that they will refuse to sanction.

(Tzu Kung asked: "What would you say of the man
Who is liked by all his fellow townsmen?"
"That is not sufficient," was the reply.
"In that case, what would you say of him who
Is hated by all his fellow townsmen?"
"Nor is that sufficient," was the reply.
"What is better is that the good among
The townsmen like him, and the bad hate him.")

The true gentleman is easy to serve
Yet difficult to please. If you attempt
To please him in any improper way,
He will be displeased. But when hiring men,
He has regard to their capacity.
The inferior man is hard to serve,
Yet easy to please. Attempt to please him,
Even improperly, he will be pleased.
But in appointing men in their work, he
Expects them to be fit for everything.

The well-bred are dignified, not pompous.
The ill-bred are pompous, not dignified.

Anyone who is earnest in spirit
Persuasive in speech, with gracious bearing,
May be called an educated person.

When a good man has trained the people for
Seven years, they might be fit to bear arms.

To lead an untrained population to
A war may be called throwing them away.

When his country is ill-governed, to be
Thinking only of pay, is dishonor.

The scholar whose regard is his comfort
Is unworthy to be deemed a scholar.

When law and order prevail in the land,
A man may be bold in speech and action.
Lacking law and order, though he may take
Action, he should lay restraint on his speech.

Men of old studied for self-improvement.
Men today study to seek approval.

("What do you think about the principle
Of rewarding enmity with kindness?"
"And with what, then, would you reward kindness? –
Reward enmity with just treatment and
Then you may reward kindness with kindness.")

Cultivate yourself to ease people's lot.

To not enlighten one who is able
To be enlightened, is to waste a man;
To try to enlighten one who is not
Able to receive it, is to waste words.

The intelligent waste not men, nor words.

Who heeds not the future will find sorrow.

It is all vain! I have never yet seen
A man fond of virtue as of beauty.

If he does not ask, "What am I to make
Of this?" and "What am I to make of that?"
Then there is nothing I can make of him.

(The Master remarked: "The noble man is
Pained over his own incompetency;
He is not pained that others ignore him.")

Noble men seek what they want in themselves.
The inferior man seeks it from others.

("Is there any word," asked Tzu Kung, "which could
Be adopted as a rule of conduct?"
"Is it not reciprocity? – Do not
To others what you would not like yourself.")

I can remember days when recorders
Left temporary blanks in their records;
When a man would lend his horse to others.
Now, such a condition no more exists.

Plausible words confound morals. Trifling
Impatience may confound a great project.

Though all hate a man, one must look into
The cause, and even though they all like him,

One must also investigate the cause.

To err and not change may be called error.

Wise men are anxious about their duty
Not about hunger, nor their poverty.

He on whom a moral duty devolves
Should not give way even to his master.

In teaching, there should be no class difference.

There are three errors to be avoided
When in the presence of a superior:
To speak before called upon – forwardness;
Not to speak when called on – timidity;
To speak before noting a superior's
Mood and expression, which is called blindness.

The wise man has nine points of thoughtful care.
In looking, care to observe distinctly;
In listening, to apprehend clearly;
In appearance, he cares to be kindly;
In manner, he cares to be courteous;
In his speaking, to be conscientious;
In duties, his care is to be earnest;
In doubt, he cares to seek information;
In anger, he cares for consequences;
And when he has the opportunity
For gain, his care is whether it is right.

Duke Ching of Ch'I had a thousand horses
But on the day of his death, his people

Knew of no virtue for which to praise him.
Po-I and Shu-Ch'I who starved to death at
The foot of Shou-Yang are still praised today.

It is only the very wisest and
The very stupidest who never change.

Love of kindness, without a love to learn,
Will find itself obscured by foolishness.
Love of knowledge, without a love to learn,
Finds itself obscured by speculation.
Love of honesty, without love to learn,
Finds itself obscured by harmful candor.
Love of straight-forwardness, without learning
Finds itself obscured by wayward judgment.
Love of daring, without a love to learn,
Finds itself obscured by indiscipline.
Love of character, without love to learn,
Finds itself obscured by intransigence.

Your honest countryman is the spoiler
Of morals.

To proclaim on the road that which you hear
Along the way is virtue thrown away.

("I wish I could proceed without speaking,"
said the Master. "If you did not speak, sir,"
said Tzu Kung, "what should we students pass on?"
"What speech has Heaven?" replied the Master.
"The four seasons do run their courses and
All things flourish; yet what speech has Heaven?")

How hard is the case of the man who stuffs
Himself with food the livelong day, never
Applying his mind to anything else.
Are there no checkers or chess games to play?
Even those games are better than nothing.

Different from these, with me there is no
Inflexible "thou shalt" or "thou shalt not."

The Emperor
The Meditations of Marcus Aurelius

Marcus Aurelius lived from 121 to 180 A.D., and was Roman emperor from 161 to the end of his life. He was the last in a line of emperors that had been the adopted heirs of their predecessors. Rather than ascending the throne by birthright, he was chosen as the most able individual, as had the previous four emperors. This era of adopted emperors represented the height of the Roman Empire and its most stable period. Unfortunately, Marcus Aurelius' successor was his son, Commodus, who was an unmitigated disaster on the throne. Aurelius' odd choice to allow his incompetent son to inherit such power led to the theory – popularized by the movie *Gladiator* – that Commodus contrived a way to secure power for himself before his father could declare another heir.

The reign of Marcus Aurelius was a troubled one. Much as he wanted to focus on improving the empire through domestic measures, he was forced to spend most of his time on the battlefield defending the empire's frontiers. Despite facing such challenges, he took time to engage in self-examination in between battles. His meditations are these reflections, and by all indications they were not meant for a public audience. Though clearly representative of the Stoic tradition preferred by the Roman aristocracy, there are features to his ideas that are uniquely his, and that made them popular among the Christians he attempted to suppress.

Because the text is a collection of personal thoughts and frustrations, it is often repetitive. Marcus Aurelius struggle with very definite aspect of life and his own part in it, and he had to frequently remind himself of his principles to ensure he maintained them. The treatment that follows avoids the repetitions in favor of brevity, since the goal here is to provide an introduction to Aurelius' brand of Stoic philosophy. To fully appreciate the emperor's mindset, it is interesting to read an unabridged version of the *Meditations*. To apply the precepts to modern life, though, the selection that follows is quite thorough.

It is striking to think that an emperor, possibly the most powerful man in the world in his time, could have had such thoughts. The fact certainly challenges us to look more closely at our own lives and principles. After all, we can hardly argue that we are too busy when a very hands-on emperor found the time to.

The Meditations of Marcus Aurelius
(excerpts)

From my grandfather I learned good morals
And the moderation of my temper.
From my father's reputation and deeds,
Modesty and a manly character.
From my mother's pious beneficence,
Simplicity in my way of living.
From my great-grandfather, to have at home
The best of teachers, and to know that on
Such things, a man should spend liberally.

From my governor, to be of neither
The green nor the blue party at the games,
To endure labor, and to want little,
To work with my own hands, and to avoid
Meddling in the affairs of others.
And to resist listening to slander.

From Diognetus, to not be busy
With trifling things, and to give no credit
To the claims of the miracle-workers,
To the repeaters of incantations,
And to the driving away of demons.
And I learned to endure freedom of speech,
To be intimate with philosophy,
And to have, in youth, written dialogues.

From Rusticus, I received the sense that
My character required improvement.

From him I learned not to show myself off
As one who practices much discipline,
Or is benevolent for display's sake.
With respect to those who offended me
By words, or did me wrong, I learned to be
Easily pacified and reconciled
As soon as they show the same readiness.
I learned to read carefully, and to be
Unsatisfied with a superficial
Or hasty understanding of a book.

From Apollonius, freedom of will
And a direct steadiness of purpose,
To look to nothing except to reason,
To be the same in the worst circumstance.
As a man both resolute and yielding
And who did not withhold his instruction,
He considered his philosophical skill
To be but the smallest of his merits.

From Sextus, I learned of benevolence.
His governance of his family was
An exemplar of fatherly manner.
I learned to live conforming to nature,
And gravity without affectation,
To look after the interest of friends,
And to tolerate ignorant persons.
And he had the power of readily
Accommodating himself to all, so
Speaking with him was more agreeable
Than any flattery. At the same time,
His associates venerated him
And he could discover and order in
Intelligent and methodical ways
The principles necessary for life.

From Alexander the grammarian,
To refrain from fault-finding and to not
Reproachfully chide those who utter words
That may be barbarous or strange-sounding,
But introduce the very expression,
Suggesting that which ought to have been used.

From Fronto, I observed what great envy
And duplicity, and hypocrisy
Are in a tyrant, and that those who are
Called the Patricians are generally
Deficient in paternal affection.

From Catulus, not to be indifferent
When a friend finds fault, even without cause,
But to try to restore his confidence.

From my brother Severus, to love kin,
To love the truth, and to love justice.
From him I received the idea of
A polity with the same laws for all,
A polity governed with regard to
Equal rights and equal freedom of speech –
The idea of kingly government
Respecting above all people's freedom.
I learned from him also consistency,
And steady regard for philosophy,
A disposition to do what is good,
To give readily, to cherish good hopes,
And to believe I am loved by my friends.
And in him I observed no concealment
Of his opinions of those he condemned.
And his friends had no need to conjecture
What he wished or did not – he made it plain.

From Maximus, I learned self-government —
Not to be led aside by anything,
Cheerfulness under all circumstances,
And to do what was set without complaint.
I observed everybody believed that
He thought as he spoke, without ill intent.
He never showed amazement and surprise.
Unhurried, he never put off a task.
Nor was he seen perplexed, nor dejected,
Nor did he laugh to disguise vexation.
And, he also had the art of being
Humorous in an agreeable way.

In my adoptive father, I observed
Mildness of temper, unchanging resolve,
A love of labor and perseverance,
And a readiness to listen to those
With propositions for the common weal.
He placed himself among the citizens.
I observed, too, his careful inquiry
In all matters of deliberation.
He never stopped his investigations
Satisfied with the first appearances.
Able to foresee things a long way off,
He provided for the smallest with ease.
Quick to check applause and all flattery,
He patiently endured blame he received.
He was not superstitious with respect
To the gods, nor did he court men by gifts.

Of the things that add to convenience,
Which fortune gives in abundant supply,
He used without arrogance or excuse
So that when he had them, he enjoyed them.

When he had them not, he did not want them.

Honoring all the true philosophers,
He did not reproach those who pretended
Nor yet was he easily led by them.
He took reasonable care of his health
Not as one who was so attached to life,
Nor with regard to personal appearance,
And yet, so that through his own attention,
He seldom needed the physician's art.

Without envy, he readily gave way
To those possessing particular knowledge,
And gave them his help, that each might enjoy
Reputation according to deserts.

He showed prudence and economy in
Exhibition of public spectacles
And the construction of public buildings.

That which was said of Socrates might be
Applied to him – that he was able both
To abstain from, and to enjoy, those things
Which many are too weak to abstain from
And cannot enjoy in moderation.

To the gods, I am indebted, having
Good grandfathers, good parents and teachers,
A good sister, good kinsmen, and good friends.
Further, I owe it to the gods that I
Was not hurried into any offense
Though I once had a disposition that,
With opportunity, I might have done.

I am thankful that I was subjected

To a ruler and a father who was
Able to take away all pride from me –
To bring me to learn it is possible
For men to live in a palace without
Desiring either guards or fancy dress,
Torches and statues and ostentation.

I thank the gods that my children have not
Been stupid, nor deformed in the body,
That I received clear, frequent impressions
About living according to nature,
And that I have never done anything
Of which I had occasion to repent.
That though my mother's fate was to die young,
She spent the last years of her life with me.
That whenever I wished to help a man
I was never told that I lacked the means..
That I have good masters for my children.

Start the morning by saying to yourself,
I shall meet with all the busybodies,
The ungrateful, arrogant, deceitful,
The envious, and the antisocial.
All these things happen to them by reason
Of their ignorance of good and evil.
I, who have seen the nature of the good –
That it is beautiful – and of the bad –
That it is ugly – and that of the man
Who is akin to me not just by blood,
But by sharing the same intelligence
And the same portion of divinity.
Not one of them can truly injure me,
For no one can fix on me what is bad.
Nor can I be angry with my kinsmen,
For we are made for cooperation

Like feet, like hands, like the rows of our teeth.
It is contrary to nature to hate.

I am but little flesh and breath and mind.
It is not allowed to be distracted.
Knowing that it will die, despise the flesh.
See that the breath is also inconstant –
Every moment sent out and sucked back in.
Considering the third, the ruling part,
No longer let this be a slave to whims,
No longer be pulled by puppeteer strings,
No longer be either dissatisfied
With the present or shrink from the future.

All of nature is significant.
Even chance is not parted from nature,
But is part of the natural order.
From thence all things flow, and what nature brings
Serves to maintain all of the universe.

Remember how long you have put off things –
How often you had opportunities.
You must now perceive of what universe
And from what order your existence flows,
And that your time is limited and fixed.
If you fail to clear away your mind's clouds,
The time will go, and will never return.

Always think steadily as a Roman,
And do what you have in hand with perfect,
Simple dignity, freedom, and justice.
Give yourself relief form all other thoughts.
Do every act as if it were your last –
Laying aside all carelessness, self-love,
Passionate aversion from your reason,

Hypocrisy, and discontent with what
Portion, by chance, has been given to you.
See how few the things are which, if possessed,
Enable men to live a quiet life,
Alike to the existence of the gods.

Do things that fall upon you distract you?
Allow time to learn something new and good,
And cease to be whirled around aimlessly.
Also avoid going the other way.
Those who do are triflers who are wearied
In life by their pointless activity.

Failure to observe another's thinking
Has seldom made a person unhappy.
But those not seeing movements of their own
Must of necessity be unhappy.

This is what you must always bear in mind:
What is the nature of the whole, and what
Is my nature — how are they related —
What kind of part, and what kind of whole.
And remember that no one hinders you
From always doing and saying the things
That conform to nature, and to your part.

There is obvious truth to the statement
By Monimus that "all is opinion."
And obvious, too, is its usefulness
If a man profits from it, in its truth.

The soul of man does violence to itself
First of all, when it becomes an abscess —
It is a tumor on the universe
When we separate ourselves from nature.

In the next place, when it turns away from,
Or turns towards to injure, any man.
Thirdly, the soul harms itself when it is
Overpowered by pleasure or by pain.
Fourth, when it playacts or is insincere.
Fifth, when it allows any of its acts
To be without aim, or done thoughtlessly.

We must make haste, not only because we
Are daily nearer to death, but also
Because our conception of many things
And understanding of them ceases first.

Observe, even things which follow after
The things produced according to nature
Contain something pleasing and attractive.
The splitting of the surface of baked bread
Contrary to the baker's art's purpose
Excites a desire for eating it.
Since they follow from things formed by nature,
They help adorn them, and they please the mind.
For one with insight with respect to things,
None of these by-products will fail to please.
He will see the real gaping jaws of beasts
With no less pleasure than those that painters
And sculptors show by their imitations.
And in an old woman and an old man,
He will see a certain maturity.
And the attractiveness of young people
He is able to look on with chaste eyes.
Many such things will seem to him pleasing
If he is familiar with nature's works.

Hippocrates, after curing many
Diseases, himself, too, fell sick and died.

Alexander and Pompey and Caesar
After often destroying whole cities,
And in battle cutting to pieces tens
Of thousands of knights and infantrymen,
Themselves, too, at last departed from life.
Heraclitus, after speculating
On the universe's conflagration
Was filled with water and smeared all over.
And lice also destroyed Democritus,
And other lice also killed Socrates.
What does all this mean? You have embarked on,
Made the voyage, and come to shore; get out.
If indeed to another life, then fine,
But if to a state without sensation,
Pains and pleasures will cease to enthrall you.
You cease to be a slave to the vessel
Which is as much clearly inferior
As that which serves it is superior:
For one is intelligent and holy
And the other is dirt and corruption

Do not waste the remainder of your life
In thoughts about others if your thinking
Lacks some hold on common utility
For you lose the chance to do something else.
What is such a person doing, and why,
What is he saying, what is he thinking,
What is he contriving, and everything
That allows our thinking to run away –
We ought to check in our series of thoughts
Everything without purpose and useless,
But most of all the overcurious
And the malignant or the suspicious.
Think only of those things about which if
One should ask: what are you thinking about?

With perfect openness you might answer
So that from your words it should be plain that
Everything in you is benevolent,
As would befit a social animal.
When such a man comes to the fore, he is
Like a priest and minister of the gods
So that he is unattached to pleasure,
Unharmed by all pain, untouched by insult.
He is a fighter in the noblest fight,
Not overpowered by any passion,
Dyed deep with justice, his soul accepting
Everything that happens, and his portion,
And only with greatest necessity
For the general good imagining
What another might mean, or do, or think.
His activity concentrates upon
His duties, and he makes his own acts fair.
He remembers that every rational
Animal is his kinsman, and to care
For all men according to man's nature.

Labor willingly and diligently
And aware of the common interest.
Do not let studied ornament distract
And be not either a man of many
Words, or busy about too many things.
And let the deity within you be
The guardian of a living being,
Firm, engaged in matters political,
Who has taken to his post like a man,
Ready to go, having need neither of
Oath nor of any man's testimony.
Do not seek from others a crutch, even
The ease they offer. A man then must stand
Erect, not be kept erect by others.

If you find in human life anything
Better than justice, truth, and fortitude,
And anything better than your own mind's
Self-satisfaction in the things that it
Enables you to do with right reason,
If you see anything better than this
Turn to it with all your soul and enjoy
That which you discovered to be the best.
But if you find everything else smaller –
Of less value – give place to nothing else.
If you diverge from this divinity
And succumb to the appetites, then you
Will be unable to concentrate on
That good thing which is most deeply your own.
It is not right that anything other
Such as praise from the many, or power,
Or enjoyment of pleasure, should compete
With anything that is rationally,
Or politically, or practically good.
Though the distractions may adapt themselves
To the better things in a small degree,
They in fact subjugate reason at once.
Freely chase the better and hold to it.

Consider nothing as profitable
That compels you to break your promises,
To lose self-respect, to hate any man,
To suspect, curse, or act the hypocrite.

Revere the faculty that produces
Your opinion, which promises freedom
From hasty judgment, friendship toward men,
And obedience to divinity.

Bear in mind that every man lives only
In the present – an invisible point –
That all the rest of his life is either
Past, or is uncertain. Brief is man's life,
And small the nook of the earth where he lives.
Brief, too, is the longest posthumous fame,
Buoyed only by a succession of poor
Human beings who will very soon die
And who know little of themselves, much less
Of someone who died a long time ago.

Make for yourself a definition or
Description of things presented to you
To see distinctly what kind of a thing
It is in substance, in its nudity.
Tell yourself its proper name, and the names
Of the things of which it was compounded,
And those into which it will be resolved.
Nothing promotes elevation of mind
As the ability to examine,
Methodically and truly, every
Object presented to you in your life.
Look at things to simultaneously
See what manner of universe this is,
And what king of use everything performs,
And what value each and everything has
With reference to the whole and to man.

And to the body belongs sensations;
To soul, appetites; to intelligence,
Principles. As physicians always have
Their instruments and knives ready in case
Their skills are in that moment required,
So do you have principles ready for
Understanding things divine and human,

And for doing everything with knowledge
Of bonds uniting divine and human.

Reason acting according to nature
Will always adapt itself easily
To what is possible and is present.

Men seek retreats for themselves, like houses
In the country, seashores, and the mountains.
You, too, are wont to desire such things,
But this desire is altogether
A mark of the most common sort of man.
For it is in your power whenever
You choose to retire into yourself.
There is no retreat that is quieter
Or freer from trouble than your own soul.
Constantly give to yourself this retreat.

If the intellectual is common
To all men, so is rationality.
If this is so, conscience must be common.
If this is so, there is a common law.
If this is so, we are co-citizens
And this world is in a manner a state.

All that which does not make a man worse than
He was, also does not make his life worse.

Do not share the opinion of things
Of he who has done, or wishes, you wrong,
Nor whatever he wishes you to think.

A man should hold in his mind these two rules:
To do only whatever the reason
May suggest is to man's utility.

The other, to change your opinion if
Anyone convinces and sets you right.
But this change of opinion must proceed
Only from a genuine conviction
It is just or of common advantage.

Do you have reason? Why then not use it?

You have existed as a part and you
Shall disappear in that which produced you.

Grains of frankincense on the same altar –
One falls before, another falls after,
But between them, it makes no difference.

Within ten days you will seem a god to
Those to whom you are now a beast and ape
If you will return to your principles,
Adhering to the worship of reason.

How much trouble he avoids who does not
Look to see what his neighbor says or thinks.
Look not 'round at others' depraved morals
But run straight along the line without pause.

Everything harmonizes with me which
Is harmonious to you, Universe.
For me, nothing is too early or late
If it is in due time for you, Nature.

Either the universe is well-arranged
Or else a chaos huddled together
Which is regardless still a universe.
But can a definite order subsist
In you, and yet disorder in the All?

Observe constantly that all things take place
By change, and accustom yourself to think
That the nature of the universe loves
Nothing so much as to change things that are,
And to make new things similar to them.

What is evil to you does not subsist
In the ruling principles of others.
It is in that part of you in which lives
The ability to form opinions.
Let this power not form such judgments
Of either bad or good, and all is well.

Constantly regard the universe as
One living being, having one substance,
One soul, to which all things have reference.

Time is like a river made up of all
Events that happen, and a violent stream,
For at the instant a thing has been seen,
It goes away, and another comes in.
And this will be carries away as well.

In the morning, when reluctant to rise,
Let this thought be present: I am rising
To do the work of a human being.
Why am I dissatisfied if I am
Going to do things for which I exist
And for which I was brought into the world?
Of have I been made just for this, to lie
Under the blankets and keep myself warm?
This is more pleasant. Do you exist, then,
For pleasure and not at all for action?
Do you not see the little plants, birds, ants,

Spiders, and bees working to give order
To their separate parts of the universe?
And are you lazy to do human work?
But it is necessary to take rest –
Necessary, however nature has
Fixed bounds on this, and also on eating
And drinking, yet you go beyond these bounds.
You do not love yourself, for if you did,
You would love your nature and nature's will.

Judge all words and deeds that are fit for you
And be not diverted by words of blame.
If it is good to do or say something,
Do not think it unworthy of yourself.

One man, doing service to another
Readily sets it down as a favor.
Another is not ready to do this,
But still thinks of the man as his debtor.
A third does not even know what he did,
But is like a vine that had produced grapes
And seeks nothing more than its proper fruit.
As a horse running, a dog tracking game,
And a bee when it has made the honey,
So a man when he has done a good act
Does not call for others to come and see,
But he goes on to do another act,
As a vine produces again the grapes.

Do not be disgusted, discouraged, or
Dissatisfied if you do not succeed
In doing everything in accordance
With right principles. But when you have failed,
Return once again, and be content if
The greater part of what you do is good

And is consistent with human nature.

Things are so shrouded that they have seemed to
Philosophers — and not just the base ones —
Altogether unintelligible —
Difficult to grasp, even to Stoics.
And all our assertions about these things
Are changeable — about short-lived objects —
For where is the man who never changes?

I am composed of the formal and the
Material, and neither will perish
Into an ultimate nonexistence.
Every part of me will be reduced by
Change into some part of the universe,
And that will change into another part,
And so on forever. By consequence
Of such change, I exist, and my parents,
And so on in the other direction.

Are you angry with him whose armpits stink?
Are you angry with him whose mouth smells foul?
And what good will this anger do for you?
He has such a mouth, he has such armpits —
Such emanations necessarily
Must come from such things. But man has reason.
And it will be said that he is able,
If he cares, to learn wherein he offends.
Well, you too have the rationality
To stir up his reason, admonish him,
And show him his error. If he listens,
You will cure him with no need for anger.

Do not be carried by things' appearance.
Instead, give help to all according to

Your own ability and their fitness.

Obedient and compliant is the
Substance of the universe. The reason
That governs it has no cause for evil,
Nor does it do evil to anything.
For it has no malice, and harms nothing
But according to it, all things are made.

Let it make no diff'rence to you whether
You are cold or warm doing your duty,
Whether drowsy or satisfied with sleep,
Whether you are ill-spoken of or praised,
Whether dying or doing something else.

Look within. Let neither the quality
Of anything, nor its value, be missed.

All existing things soon change. They will be
Reduced to vapor, or will be dispersed.

The best way of avenging yourself is
Avoid becoming like the wrongdoer.

Motions and changes continually
Renew the world, just as the course of time
Produces the duration of ages.
In this flowing stream, then, where is the thing
On which any man would set a high price.
It would be as if a man should fall in
Love with one of the sparrows that fly by
When it has already passed out of sight.
Of this kind is the very life of man
For such as it is to have once drawn air
And to give it back in every moment

As is the whole of your respiration
Which you received at birth, to give it back
To the element from which you drew it.

How strangely men act. They will not praise those
Who are living at the same time as them.
But to be praised by the posterity –
By those they have never seen or ever
Will see – they set great value on such praise.

If it is difficult to accomplish
Something yourself, do not think that it is
Impossible for man. But if something
Is possible for man, think that this, too,
Can be attained by you – within your reach.

If a man is able to convince me
And show me I do not think or act right,
I will gladly change, for I seek the truth
And by that no man was ever injured.
He who abides in error is injured.

As to animals that have no reason,
And generally all things and objects,
Make use of them with liberal spirit.
But toward human beings, since they have
Reason, behave in a social spirit.

Alexander the Macedonian
And his groom were in the same state by death –
Either received by the same principles
Or alike dispersed among the atoms.

If any man should ask you how the name
Antoninus is written, would you, with

A straining of voice, utter each letter?
And what if the questioner grew angry.
Would you be angry, too? Would you not go
On, composed, and spell out every letter?
Just so, then, in this life also recall
That every duty is made up of parts.
And in fulfilling each part of duties,
Show no anger to those angry with you.

Death is a cessation of impressions
Through the senses, and the pulling of strings
That move the appetites, and the movements
Of the thoughts, and of service to the flesh.

It is a shame for the soul to give way
In this life, when your body has not yet.

How many pleasures have been enjoyed by
The robbers, patricides, and the tyrants.

Frequently consider the connection
Of everything in the universe and
Of their relation to one another.
In a way, all things are implicated
With one another, and all in this way
Are friends and companions to each other.

If you suppose things not in your power
Are good or bad for you, then suffering
A bad thing or the loss of a good thing,
You will blame the gods and hate men, as well –
Those who are the cause of the misfortune,
Or those suspected of being the cause.
And indeed we do a great injustice
When we dwell upon the finding of fault.

If we judge only things in our power
To be good or bad, there is no reason
For finding fault with the gods or with men.

All are working together to one end —
Some with knowledge and design, and others
Not knowing what they do, like sleeping men
Who are, according to Heraclitus,
Laborers and cooperators in
The things that take place in the universe.
But men cooperate in different ways.
It remains, then, for you to understand
Among what kind of men you place yourself.

Does the sun undertake to do rain's work,
Or Aesculapius the work of earth?
Is not each star different yet working with
The others toward the very same end?

When you wish to delight yourself, then think
Of the virtues of those who live with you.
Nothing delights so much as examples
Of virtues when they are exhibited
In the morals of those who live with us.

He who loves fame considers his own good
As from another man's activity.
He who loves pleasure, his own sensations.
But he who loves only understanding
Considers his own acts to be his good.

Accustom yourself to attend with care
To all that is said by another and
As much as it is possible for you,
Try to put yourself in the speaker's mind.

To the jaundiced, honey tastes bitter, and
To those with rabies, water causes fear.
Do you think that a false opinion has
Less power than the bile or the poison?

How can principles become dead unless
Thoughts relating to them are extinguished?
But it is in your power to fan these
Thoughts continuously into a flame.

The idle business of show, plays on stage,
Flocks of sheep, herds, exercises with spears,
A bone cast to little dogs, bits of bread
Into fish ponds, the laboring of ants,
Runnings about of frightened little mice,
Puppets pulled by strings – they are all alike.
It is your duty in the midst of such
To show good humor and not a proud air.
Understand, though, that every man is worth
Just as the things with which he is busy.

In discourse, you must attend to what is
Said, in action, you must see what is done.
In the latter, see the intended end.
In the former, see what is signified.

Do not be ashamed to be helped. It is
Your business to perform your duty like
A soldier in the assault on a town.
What if, being lame, you cannot mount up
The battlements alone, but can with help?

Is there any human afraid of change?
And yet, what can take place without changes?

What, then, is more suitable to nature?
And how can you take a hot bath unless
The wood for fire undergoes a change?
Can you be nourished unless food changes?
Can something useful be done without change?
Do you not see, then, that for yourself, too,
Change must be equally necessary,
As it is for universal nature?

Look around at the courses of the stars
As if you were going along with them,
And constantly consider the changes
Of the elements into each other,
For such thoughts purge the filth of earthly life.

Look within, where the fountain of good is.
It will ever bubble up, if you dig.

In every pain let this thought he present –
There is no dishonor in it, nor does it
Make the governing intelligence worse.
Indeed, in the case of most pains, let this
Remark of Epicurus be your guide –
That pain is neither intolerable
Nor everlasting if you bear in mind
That it has its limits, as long as your
Imagination adds nothing to it.

Take care that you avoid feeling toward
The inhuman as they feel toward men.

Nature has not so mixed intelligence
With the composition of the body
As not to have allowed you the power
Of circumscribing yourself, of bringing

Under subjection all that is your own.
For it is possible to be divine
And to be recognized as such by none.

The perfection of moral character
Consists in this: in passing every day
As if it were the last, and also in
Being neither violently excited,
Nor torpid, nor playing the hypocrite.

It is ridiculous for any man
Not to fly from his own badness, which is
Indeed possible, but to fly from that
Of other men, which is impossible.

Whatever the rational and social
Faculty finds to be neither social
Nor intelligent, it rightly judges
To be quite inferior to itself.

Having done a good act, which was received,
Why do you look for a third thing besides,
Either the reputation of having
Done that good, or to obtain a return?

On the occasion of every act ask
How will this be with respect to me? And
Will I regret it? What more do I seek
If what I am doing now is the work
Of an intelligent living being.

Alexander and Caesar and Pompey —
What are they in comparison with men
Like Diogenes and Heraclitus
And Socrates? For the latter three

Were acquainted with things, and their causes,
And with their matter. And the principles
Ruling over all these men were the same.
But as to the former, how many things
Had they to care for, and were they slaves to.

Consider that men will do the same things
Even though you would burst with rage at them.

Repentance is a kind of self-reproof
For having neglected something useful.
That which is good must be something useful
And the better man should look after it.

Constantly and, if it be possible,
On the occasion of each impression,
Apply to it the solid principles
Of physics, ethics, and dialectics.

Remember that it is a shame to be
Surprised if the fig tree produces figs.
And just so it is to be surprised if
The world makes such and such things which it makes.
And for the physician and the helmsman,
It is truly a shame to be surprised
If a man has a fever or unease,
Or if the wind is unfavorable.

Remember that to change your opinion
And to follow him who corrected you
Is as consistent with your freedom as
It is to still persist in your error.

Attend to what is before you, whether
An opinion or an act or a word.

If you choose to become good tomorrow
And not good today, you suffer justly.

Receive wealth or prosperity without
Arrogance. Be ready to let it go.

If you have ever seen a hand cut off,
Or a foot, or a head lying apart
Far from the rest of a person's body,
So does a man make himself, as he can,
Who is not content with what happens and
Separates from others unsocially.

Remember that the ruling faculty
Is invincible when, self-collected,
It is wholly satisfied with itself,
If it does nothing that it does not choose,
Even resisting from obstinacy.
What then will it be when it forms judgments
About anything, aided by reason?
Therefore, the mind that is free from passions
Is a citadel, for man has nothing
More secure to which he flies for refuge.
He who does not see this is ignorant,
But he who has seen it and does not fly
To this refuge is surely unhappy.

Neither in your actions be too sluggish
Nor in conversation without method
Nor wandering aimlessly in your thoughts
Nor let there be in your soul an inward
Contention nor external effusion,
Nor be so busy that you lack leisure.

Do you wish to be praised by a person
Who curses himself three times each hour?
To please a man who does not please himself?
Does a person please himself who repents
Of nearly everything that he has done?

Men exist for the sake of each other.
You either teach them, then, or bear with thm.

Enter into every man's faculty,
And also let all others enter yours.

Injustice is impiety. For since
The universal nature has made us
Rational animals for other's sake –
To help each other according to need
But in no way to injure one another –
He who transgresses her will is guilty
Of impiety to divinity.
And the liar, too, is just as guilty
To that same highest of divinities
Because if the universal nature
Is the nature of all the things that are,
And this universal nature is truth
And the prime cause of all things that are true
Then he who lies intentionally is
Guilty of impiety inasmuch
As he acts unjustly by deceiving,
And he who lies unintentionally
Is guilty inasmuch as he is at
Variance with universal nature,
And inasmuch as he disturbs order
By fighting against the world's own nature
When he has been endowed by that nature
With the means to distinguish false from true.

Failing to use them, he lost the power.
Indeed, he who pursues pleasure as good
And avoids pain as evil is guilty.
For certainly such a man must often
Find fault with the universal nature,
Alleging it assigns to bad and good
Things that are contrary to their deserts.
For frequently the bad enjoy pleasure
And possess the things that procure pleasure,
But the good have pain and things causing pain.
He who pursues pleasure will not abstain
From injustice – plainly impiety.

He who does wrong, does wrong against himself.
He who acts unjustly, acts unjustly
To himself, because he makes himself bad.

All that share in a common element
Have an affinity for their own kind.
Only intelligent animals have
Now forgotten this common desire,
And in them alone the property of
Flowing together seems not to be seen.
But though men strive to avoid this union
They are still caught and held strongly by it
For their nature is too potent for them.

Penetrate into a man's principles
And you see what judge you are afraid of
And what kind of judge he is of himself.

Where is the harm or strangeness in the boor
Acting like a boor? See whether you are
Not yourself more to blame, not expecting
That he would err in such a common way.

You had the reason to guess it likely
Yet you have forgotten and are amazed.

When you have assumed these names – good, modest,
Truthful, rational, magnanimous, and
A man of equanimity – take care
That you do not alter or lose these names.
Should you lose them, quickly return to them.
And remember that the term 'rational'
Was intended to signify to us
A discriminating attention to all
Objects, and a freedom from negligence.
Equanimity is voluntary
Acceptance of the things assigned to you.
Magnanimity is elevation
Of the reasoning faculty above
The pleasure or pain sensations of flesh,
And above that poor thing called fame, and death.
If you maintain possession of these names
Without desiring to hear them addressed
To you by others, you will enter on
Another life and be another man.
To continue to be such as you are
And to be torn in pieces and defiled
Is the character of a stupid man
And one overfond of his meager life
Like those half-devoured wild beast fighters
Who, though covered with wounds and gore, still beg
That they be kept to the following day,,
Though they will be exposed to the same state.
Fix yourself in possession of these names
If you are able to abide in them,
Abide as if on Isles of the Blessed.
If you feel adrift, without a firm hold,
Then go courageously into some nook

Where you can maintain them, not in passion,
But with simplicity and modesty.
In remembrance of these names, it will help
Greatly if you remember, too, the gods,
And that they do not wish to be flattered,
But wish all beings be made like themselves.

A spider is proud when catching a fly,
One man when he has caught a poor hare,
Another when he has a fish in net,
Another when he has taken wild boars,
And another when he has taken bears,
And another then taking Sarmatians.
Are not these robbers, by their opinions?

Why should there be need of suspicious fear
Since it is certainly in your power
To inquire on what ought to be done.
If you see clearly, go by it content;
If you do not see, take the best advice.
But if any other things oppose you
Proceed on with due consideration,
Keeping to that which appears to be just.

To her who gives and takes back all – Nature –
The man who is learned and modest says,
"Give what you will and take back what you will."
And he says this without pride, but rather
Obediently and well-pleased with her.

Constantly contemplate the whole of time
And the whole of substance, and consider
That all individual things compared
To substance are a seed of a fig, and
As to time, the turning of a gimlet.

Consider what humans are when they eat,
Sleep, couple, evacuate, and so forth.
Then what kind of person they are when they
Are imperious and arrogant or
Angry — scolding from elevated place.
But a short time ago, to how many
Things were they slaves, and for what things were they?

In all you do, pause and ask if death Is
Dreadful because it deprives you of it.

Let it not be in any man's power
To say truly that you are not simple
Or that you are not good. If anyone
Thinks this of you, let him be a liar.
This is altogether in your power.

There is no man so fortunate that
There shall not be, when he is dying, some
Who are pleased with what is soon to happen.
Do not, however, for this reason go
Away less kindly disposed toward them.

Have I done something for the general
Interest? Well then, I have my reward.
Keep this thought, and never stop doing such good.

How plain does it appear that there is not
Another condition of life so well
Suited for philosophizing as this
In which you, perchance, now happen to be.

As those who try to stand in your way when
You proceed according to right reason

Will not be able to turn you aside,
So neither let them drive you from feeling
Benevolently toward them. But be
On your guard equally in both matters –
Not only in your judgment and action,
But also in being gentle to all.

No nature is inferior to art
For arts imitate the nature of things.

Men despise and flatter one another.
Men wish to raise themselves above others,
And also crouch before one another.

Unsound and insincere is he who
Says, "I have determined to deal with you
In a fair way." What are you doing, man?
There is no reason to give this notice.
It will soon enough show itself by acts.

If any offend you, consider first:
What is my relation to other men
And that we are made for one another.
Second, ponder what kind of men they are
At the table, in their bed, and so forth –
Especially, under what compulsions
They operate, and with what pride they act.
Third, that if men do rightly what they do,
We ought not to be displeased, but if they
Do wrong, it is plainly in ignorance.
Fourth, consider that you also do wrong,
And that you are yet a man like others.
And, even abstaining from certain faults,
Have the disposition to commit them.
Fifth, consider that you do not even

Understand whether men are doing wrong
For many things are done by circumstance.
A man must learn a great deal to allow
Him to pass correct judgment on others.
Sixth, consider when you are vexed or grieved
That a man's life is only a moment.
Seventh, that men's acts are not what disturbs,
But rather it is our own opinions
Which, if removed, take with them our anger.
Eighth, consider how much more pain is brought
On us by the anger and vexation
Than by the acts that disturbed us themselves.
Ninth, consider that good disposition
Is invincible, if genuine and
Not an affected smile and acted part.
Remember these nine rules, as if you had
Received them as a gift from the Muses,
And begin to be a man while you live.
If you will, receive also a tenth gift
From Apollo, leader of the Muses:
To expect bad men not to do wrong is
Madness, and an impossibility,
But to allow men to behave so to
Others, and not expect them to wrong you
Is irrational and tyrannical.

He who had not one and always the same
Object, the same purpose, in life, cannot
Remain one and the same all through his life.

The Pythagoreans bid us to look
To the heavens that we may remember
Those bodies that always do the same things
And in the same manner perform their work,
And of their purity and nudity,

For there is no veil covering a star.

Neither in your writing nor in reading
Will you be able to lay down the rules
For others before learning to obey
Rules yourself. Much more is this so in life.

You are composed of three things: body, breath,
And intelligence. Of these the first two
Are yours insofar as to care for them
Is your duty. The third is truly yours.

I have often wondered how it is that
Every man loves himself more than all
The rest of mankind, yet sets less value
On his own opinion of himself than
He does on the opinion of others.

How ridiculous and what a stranger
He is who is surprised at anything.

If it is not right, then do not do it.
If it is not true, then do not say it.
Let your impulse be in your own power.

Perceive you have in you something better
And more divine than causes of effects
That, as it were, pull on you by the strings.

The security of life is in this:
To examine everything thoroughly —
What it is itself, what the formal part,
What is its material. With all your
Soul, to do justice and to say the truth.
What remains except to enjoy your life

By joining one good thing to another,
To leave not even small gaps in between.

The Prince
The Dhammapada of The Buddha

Siddhartha Gautama, known as the Buddha (awakened one), lived in Northern India in the 6th century B.C. According to the traditional account, he was a prince who became concerned about the state in which human beings lived, and sought to discover the underlying reasons for human suffering. Though called "the Buddha," it was his hope, as is clear in the Dhammapada, that there should be many Buddhas – that one day everyone could be awakened to the reality in which we find ourselves.

The Buddha advocated a middle way – a path between the self-indulgence of regular life and the self-mortification practiced by ascetics. Over the course of a long teaching career spanning five decades and involving traveling throughout ancient India, he gained a large following and established an extensive oral tradition through his lectures. That tradition was eventually committed to writing in the first century B.C. by the Fourth Buddhist Council, filling more than thirty volumes.

The *Dhammapada* is the best known portion of the canon, mainly due to the fact that it is composed of brief verses. It is also popular because the ethics espoused by it are not necessarily particular to Buddhism, but are meant to be universal. The rest of the canon tends to be more focused on the specific tenets of Buddhism. Considering the size of the canon and the centuries between the Buddha's own life and the first attempt to write it all down, there are necessarily questions about which portions of the canon were the Buddha's own words. The *Dhammapada*, because it is in the form of memorable quotes, is considered to be most likely from the lips of the prince himself.

There are different versions of the *Dhammapada*. Between them, they have around 330 verses in common. The version that follows is from the Pali canon, which is the most complete surviving canon, and the original contained 423 verses. Almost all of the verses have been reproduced here. The only exception was in the case of a handful of spiritually-oriented verses which had nothing to do with ethics.

I have left certain terms – Muni, Samana, and Brahmana – untranslated because their meaning is clear from context. They all refer to individuals on the path the Buddha is prescribing.

The Dhammapada
(excerpts)

All that we are is the result of thought:
It is founded on what we have thought and
It is furthermore made up of our thoughts.
If a man speaks or acts with evil thoughts,
Pain follows him, just as the wheel follows
The foot of the ox that draws the carriage.

All that we are is the result of thought:
It is founded on what we have thought and
It is furthermore made up of our thoughts.
If a man speaks or acts with a pure thought,
Happiness follows him like a shadow.

'He abused me, he beat me, he robbed me,
He defeated me' – in those who harbor
Thoughts such as these, hatred will never cease.

'He abused me, he beat me, he robbed me,
He defeated me' – in those who do not
Harbor thoughts such as these hatred will cease.

Because hatred does not cease by hatred
At any time: hatred ceases by love.
This is an old rule.

The world knows not that all must end here; but
Those who know it, their quarrels cease at once.

He who lives looking for pleasures only,
His senses uncontrolled, immoderate
In his food, idle, and weak — the tempter
Will certainly overthrow him with ease,
As the wind throws down a weak rooted tree.

He who lives without looking for pleasures,
His senses well controlled, moderate in
His food, faithful and strong, him the tempter
Will certainly not overthrow, any
More than the wind throws down rocky mountains.

They who imagine truth in untruth, and
See untruth in truth, never arrive at
Truth, but follow instead vain desires.

They who know truth in truth, and untruth in
Untruth, reach truth, and follow true wishes.

As rain breaks through an ill-thatched house, passion
Will break through any unreflecting mind.

As rain does not break through a well-thatched house,
Passion will not a well-reflecting mind.

The evil-doer mourns in this world, and
He mourns in the next; he mourns and suffers
When he sees the evil of his own work.

The virtuous man delights in this world,
And he delights in the next; he delights
In both. He delights and rejoices, when
He sees the purity of his own work.

The evil-doer suffers in this world,
And he suffers in the next. He suffers
Thinking of the evil he has done and
Suffers more going on the evil path.

The virtuous man has happiness in
This world, and he is happy in the next;
He is happy in both. He is happy
Thinking of the good he has done and still
More happy when going on the good path.

The thoughtless man, even if able to
Recite a large portion of the law, but
Is not a doer of it, has no share
In the priesthood, but is like a cowherd
Who is counting the cattle of others.

The follower of the law, even if
He can recite only a small portion,
Having forsaken passion and hatred
And foolishness, possesses true knowledge
And serenity of mind, he, caring
For nothing in this world or that to come,
Has indeed a full share in the priesthood.

Earnestness is the path of Nirvana,
Meanwhile thoughtlessness is the path of death.
Those who are in full earnest do not die;
The thoughtless are as if dead already.

Those who are far advanced in earnestness,
Having understood this clearly, delight
In the earnestness, and rejoice in the
Knowledge of the Ariyas, the noble.

These wise people, meditative, steady,
Always possessed of strong powers, attain
To Nirvana, the highest happiness.

If an earnest person has roused himself,
If he is not forgetful, if his deeds
Are pure, if he acts considerately,
If he shows restraint, and lives according
To the law, then his glory will increase.

By rousing himself, by earnestness, and
By restraint, the wise man makes for himself
An island which no flood can overwhelm.

Fools chase after vanity and evil.
Wise men keep earnestness as their best jewel.

Chase not after vanity, nor after
The enjoyment of love and lust! He who
Is earnest and thoughtful, gains ample joy.

When the learned man drives off vanity
By earnestness, he, climbing the terraced
Heights of wisdom, looks down upon the fools,
Serene he looks upon the toiling crowd,
As one on a mountain looks on the plains.

Earnest among the thoughtless, and awake
Among the sleepers, the wise man proceeds
Like a racer, leaving behind the hack.

A monk who delights in earnestness, who
Looks with fear on thoughtlessness, moves about
Like fire, burning all of his fetters.

A monk who delights in reflection, who
Looks with fear on thoughtlessness, cannot fall
Away – he is close upon Nirvana.

Just as a fletcher makes straight his arrow,
A wise man makes straight trembling, unsteady
Thought, which is hard to guard or to hold back.

It is good to tame the mind, which is hard
To hold and flighty, rushing wherever
It listeth; a tamed mind brings happiness.

Let the wise man guard his thoughts, for they are
Difficult to perceive, artful, and rush
Where they list: thoughts guarded bring happiness.

Those who bridle their mind which travels far,
Moves about alone without a body,
And hides within the chamber of the heart,
Will be free from the bonds of the tempter.

If a man's thoughts are not dissipated
If his mind is not perplexed, if he has
Ceased to think of good or evil, then there
Is no fear for him while he is watchful.

Knowing that this body is like a jar,
And making this thought firm like a fortress,
One should strike the tempter with the weapon
Of knowledge, one should watch him and not rest.

Soon this body will lie on earth, without
Understanding, as if a useless log.

Whatever a hater may do to a

Hater, or else an enemy to an
Enemy, a wrongly-directed mind
Will do to us even greater mischief.

Not a mother, not a father will do
So much, nor another; a correctly
Directed mind will do greater service.

Who shall overcome this earth, and the world
Of hell, and the world of the gods? Who shall
Find out the plainly shown path of virtue,
As a clever man finds out the flower?

The disciple will overcome the earth,
The world of hell, and the world of the gods.
The disciple will find out the plainly
Shown path of virtue, finding the flower.

He who knows that this body is like froth,
And has learnt that it is unsubstantial
As a mirage, will break the flower-point
Arrow, and never see the king of death.

Death carries away a man who gathers
Flowers and whose mind is distracted, as
A flood carries off a sleeping village.

Death subdues a man who is gathering
Flowers, and whose mind is distracted, and
Before he is satisfied by pleasures.

As the bee collects nectar and departs
Without injuring the flower, or its
Scent, so let a sage dwell in his village.

Not the perversities of others, nor
Their sins of commission or omission,
But his own misdeeds and negligences
Should a sage direct his attention to.

Like a beautiful flower, colorful
But without scent, are fine but fruitless words
From him who does not act accordingly.

But, like a beautiful flower, full of
Color and scent, are the fine and fruitful
Words of him who does act accordingly.

As many kinds of wreaths can be made from
A heap of flowers, so many good things
May be achieved by a mortal once born.

The scent of flowers travels not against
The wind, nor sandal-wood, or Tagara
And Mallikâ flowers; but the odor
Of good people travels even against
The wind; a good man pervades ev'ry place.

Sandal-wood or Tagara, a lotus,
Or a Vassikî, among these sorts of
Perfumes, that of virtue is unsurpassed.

Of the people who possess these virtues,
Who live without thoughtlessness, and who are
Emancipated through true knowledge, then
Mara, the tempter, never finds the way.

As on a heap of rubbish cast upon
The highway, the lily will grow full of
Perfume and delight, thus the disciple

Shines forth by his knowledge among all those
Who are like rubbish, walking in darkness.

Long is the night to him who is awake;
Long is a mile to him who is tired;
Long is life to those not knowing the law.

If a traveler does not meet with one
Who is his better, or else his equal,
Let him keep to solitary journey;
There is no companionship with a fool.

'These sons belong to me. This wealth belongs
To me,' with such thoughts fools are tormented.
He himself does not belong to himself;
How much less sons and wealth belong to him?

The fool who knows his foolishness, is wise
At least so far. But a fool who thinks that
He is wise, he is called a fool indeed.

If a fool be associated with
A wise man, even for the length of his
Life, he will perceive the truth as little
As a spoon perceives the taste of the soup.

If an intelligent person is for
One minute only associated
With a wise man, he will soon perceive Truth,
As the tongue perceives the taste of the soup.

Fools of little understanding have as
Their greatest enemies themselves, for they
Do evil deeds which must bear bitter fruits.

That deed is not well done of which a man
Must repent, and the reward of which he
Receives crying and with a tearful face.

No, that deed is well done of which a man
Does not repent, and the reward of which
He can receive gladly and cheerfully.

As long as the evil deed done does not
Bear fruit, the fool thinks it is like honey;
But when it ripens, then he suffers grief.

And when the evil deed, after it has
Become known, brings sorrow to the fool, then
It destroys his bright lot, nay, cleaves his head.

Let the fool wish for false reputation,
For precedence among monks, for lordship
In the convents, for worship from others!

'May both the layman and he who has left
The world think that all this is done by me;
May they be subject to me in all things
Which are to be done or not to be done,'
These are the thoughts in the mind of the fool,
And his desire and his pride increase.

If you see an intelligent man who
Tells you where true treasures are to be found,
Who shows what is to be avoided,
And administers reproofs, follow him;
It will be better for his followers.

Let him admonish, let him teach, let him
Forbid what is improper! He will be

Beloved of the good, by bad, hated.

Do not have evil-doers for your friends,
Do not have low people for your friends: have
Instead virtuous people for your friends,
Seek to have for your friends the best of men.

Well-makers lead the water and fletchers
Bend the arrow; carpenters bend a log
Of wood, and wise people fashion themselves.

As solid rock is not by wind shaken,
The wise falter not amidst blame and praise.

Good people walk on whatever befall,
The good prattle not, longing for pleasure;
Whether touched by happiness or sorrow
Wise people never seem thrilled or depressed.

If, whether for his own sake, or for the
Sake of others, a man wishes neither
For a son, nor for wealth, nor for lordship,
Nor for his own success by unfair means,
Then he is good, and wise, and virtuous.

Those whose mind is well-grounded in all the
Elements of knowledge, who cling not to
Anything, rejoice in their freedom from
Attachment, with appetites conquered, and
Are light-filled, are free even in this world.

There is no suffering for him who has
Finished his journey, and abandoned grief,
Who has freed himself on all sides and in
Every way – throwing off all fetters.

They depart with their thoughts well-collected,
They are not happy in their abode; like
Swans who have left their lake, they leave their home.

Men who have no riches, who live on food,
Who have perceived void and unconditioned
Freedom – Nirvana – their path is hard to
Understand, like that of birds in the air.

He whose appetites are stilled, who is not
Absorbed in enjoyment, who has perceived
Void and unconditioned freedom, his path
Is hard to understand, like that of birds.

Even the gods envy him whose senses,
Like horses broken in by the driver,
Have been subdued, who is free from all pride,
And who is also free from appetites.

His thought is quiet, quiet are his word
And deed, when he has obtained freedom by
True knowledge, becoming a quiet man.

In a hamlet or in a forest, and
In the deep water or on the dry land,
Wherever venerable persons dwell,
In that place it is truly delightful.

Forests are delightful; where the world finds
No delight, there the passionless will find
Delight, for they look not for base pleasures.

Even though a speech be a thousand words,
But they are all senseless, one word of sense

Is better, which if man hears, quiets him.

Even though a poem be a thousand
Words, but made up of senseless words, one word
Is better, which if man hears, quiets him.

Though a man recite a hundred poems
Made up of senseless words, one word of law
Is better, which if man hears, quiets him.

One man conquers in battle a thousand
Times thousand men, and another conquers
Himself — he is the greater conqueror.

If man for a hundred years sacrifice
Month after month with a thousand, and if
He but for one moment pay homage to
A man whose soul is grounded in knowledge,
Better is that homage than sacrifice.

If a man for a hundred years worship
Agni in the forest, and if he but
For one moment pay homage to a man
Whose soul is grounded in true knowledge, then
Better is the homage than that worship.

What a man sacrifices in this world
As an offering or an oblation
For a whole year in order to gain worth,
The whole of it is not worth a quarter;
Reverence to the righteous is better.

He who always greets and who constantly
Reveres the aged, four things will increase
To him — life, beauty, happiness, power.

But he who lives a hundred years, vicious
And unrestrained, one day is better if
A man is virtuous and reflecting.

He who lives a hundred years, ignorant
And unrestrained, one day's life is better
If a man is wise and reflecting.

And he who lives a hundred years, idle
And weak, a life of one day is better
If a man has attained firmness and strength.

He who lives a hundred years, not seeing
Beginning and end, a life of one day
Is better if a man sees start and end.

If a man would hasten towards the good,
He should keep his thought away from evil;
If a man does what is good slothfully,
Then truly his mind delights in evil.

If a man commits a sin, let him not
Do it again; let him not delight in
The sin: pain is the outcome of evil.

If a man does what is good, then let him
Do it again; let him delight in it,
For happiness is the outcome of good.

Even an evil man sees happiness
As long as his evil deed is not ripe;
But when his evil action has ripened,
Then does the evil-doer see evil.

Even a good man will see evil days,
As long as his good deed has not ripened;
But when his good deed has ripened in full,
Then does the good man see his happy days.

And let no man think lightly of evil,
Saying in his heart, It will not come nigh
Unto me. Even by the falling of
Water-droplets, a water-pot is filled;
The fool becomes full of evil, even
If he gathers it little by little.

Let no man think lightly of good, saying
In his heart, It will not come nigh to me.
Even by the falling of water-drops
A water-pot is filled; the wise man then
Becomes full of good, even if he can
Only gather it little by little.

Let a man avoid evil deeds, as a
Merchant, if he has few companions and
Carries much wealth, avoids dangerous roads;
As a man who loves life avoids poison.

He who has no wound on his hand, may touch
Poison with his hand; poison affects not
One who has no wound; nor is there evil
For the man who does not commit evil.

If a man offend a harmless, pure, and
Innocent person, the evil falls back
On that fool, like dust thrown against the wind.

Not in sky, not in the midst of the sea,
Not if we enter into mountain clefts,

Is there a spot in the entire world
Where death could not overcome the mortal.

All men tremble at punishment, all men
Love life; remember that you are like them,
And do not kill, nor cause others to die.

Do not speak harshly to anybody;
Those who are spoken to will answer you
In the same way. Angry speech is painful,
The exchange of blows for blows will touch you.

If, like a shattered gong, you utter not,
It is then that you have reached Nirvana;
And then contention is not known to you.

As a cowherd drives his cows to stable,
So do Age and Death drive the life of men.

A fool does not know it when he commits
His evil deeds, but the wicked man burns
By his own deeds, as if burnt by fire.

He who inflicts pain on innocent and
Harmless ones, will come to one of ten states:
He will have cruel suffering, loss, body
Injury, heavy affliction, or loss
Of mind, or a misfortune coming from
The king, or a fearful accusation,
Or loss of relations, or destruction
Of wealth, or lightning will burn his houses.

Not nakedness, not platted hair, not dirt,
Not fasting, or lying on the earth, not
Rubbing with dust, not sitting motionless,

Can purify one filled with desires.

And he who, though dressed in fine apparel,
Exercises tranquility, is chaste,
Subdued, restrained, and quiet, and has ceased
To find fault with all other beings, he
Indeed is a priest, and an ascetic.

Is there in this world any man restrained
By humility so that he does not
Mind reproof, as a well-trained horse the whip?

Like a well-trained horse when touched by the whip,
Be active and lively, and by faith, by
Virtue, by vigor, by meditation,
And by discernment of the law you will
Overcome this pain, perfect in knowledge
And behavior, and never forgetful.

Look at this dressed-up lump, covered with wounds,
Joined together, ever sickly, full of
Many thoughts, which has no strength and no hold!

This body is wasted, full of sickness,
And frail; as this heap of corruption
Breaks to pieces, life indeed ends in death.

Those white bones, like gourds thrown away in fall,
What pleasure is there in looking at them?

After a stronghold has been made of bones,
It is covered with flesh and blood, and there
Do dwell old age and death, pride and deceit.

The brilliant chariots of kings are

Destroyed, the body also approaches
Destruction, but the virtue of people
Never dies – thus the good say to the good.

A man who has learnt little, grows old like
An ox; flesh grows, but his knowledge does not.

Men not observing proper discipline,
And who have not gained treasure in their youth,
Perish like herons in a fishless lake.

Men not observing proper discipline,
And who have not gained treasure in their youth,
Lie, like broken bows, sighing for the past.

If a man hold himself dear, let him watch
Himself carefully; during one out of
Three watches, a wise man should be watchful.

Let each man direct himself first to what
Is proper, then let him teach the others;
In this way a wise man will not suffer.

If a man make himself as he teaches
The others to be, then, being himself
Well-subdued, he may subdue the others;
One's own self is difficult to subdue.

Self is the lord of self, who else could be?
With self well subdued, man finds a rare lord.

Evil done by oneself, self-begotten,
Self-bred, such evil crushes the foolish,
Just as a diamond breaks a precious stone.

He whose wickedness is very great brings
Himself down to that state where enemies
Wish him to be, just as any creeper
Does with the tree which it encompasses.

Bad deeds, and those deeds hurtful to ourselves,
Are easy to do; what is constructive
And good is very difficult to do.

By oneself the evil is done, by oneself
One suffers; by oneself evil is left
Undone, by oneself one is purified.
Purity and impurity belong
To oneself, none can purify others.

Let no one forget his own duty for
The sake of another's, however great;
Let a man, after he has discerned his
Duty, be always attentive to it.

He who formerly was reckless and then
Became sober, he brightens up this world,
Like the moon when it is freed from the clouds.

He whose evil deeds are covered by good,
Such a man also brightens up this world,
Like the moon when it is freed from the clouds.

If a man has transgressed one law, speaks lies,
And scoffs, there is no evil he won't do.

He whose conquest is not conquered again,
Into whose conquest no one in this world
Enters, by what track can you lead him, the
Awakened, the Omniscient, the trackless?

He whom no desire with snares can lead
Astray, by what track can you lead him, the
Awakened, the Omniscient, the trackless?

And even the gods envy those who are
Awakened and not forgetful, who are
Given to meditation, who are wise,
And who delight in repose from this world.

Difficult is the conception of men,
And difficult is the life of mortals.
Difficult is the hearing of True Law,
And difficult is the Awakened's birth.

The Awakened call patience the highest
Penance, and long-suffering the highest
Nirvana. He is not an anchorite
Who strikes, not an ascetic who insults.

Not to blame, not to strike, to live restrained
Under the law, to be moderate in
Eating, to sleep and sit alone, and to
Dwell exclusively on the highest thoughts —
This is the teaching of the Awakened.

There is no satisfying lusts, even
By a shower of gold pieces; he who
Knows that lusts satisfy only briefly
And ultimately cause pain, he is wise.

Even in heavenly pleasures he finds
No satisfaction, the disciple who
Is fully awakened delights only
In the destruction of all desires.

Men, driven by fear, go to many a
Refuge, to mountains, forests, sacred trees.

But that is not a safe refuge, nor the
Best refuge; a man is not delivered
From all pains after having gone to it.

He who takes refuge with Buddha, the Law,
And the Order; and he who, with a clear
Understanding, sees the four holy truths —
Pain, the origin of pain, destruction
Of pain, and the eightfold way that leads to
The quieting of pain — that is the safe
Refuge, that is the best refuge; having
Gone there, man is delivered from all pain.

A Buddha is not easily found, as
He is not born everywhere. Wherever
Such a sage is born, that people prospers.

Happy is the awakened's arising,
Happy is the teaching of the True Law,
Happy is the peace in the order, and
Happy is devotion of those at peace.

Let us live happily then, not hating
Those who hate us! Among men who hate us
Let us dwell, remaining free from hatred!

Let us live happily, free from ailments
Among the ailing! Among men who are
Ailing let us dwell, free from the ailments!

Let us live happily then, free from greed

Among the greedy! Among men who are
Greedy let us dwell, keeping free from greed!

Let us live happily then, though we call
Nothing our own! Then we shall truly be
Like the bright gods, feeding on happiness!

Victory breeds hatred, for the conquered
Is unhappy. He who has given up
Both victory and defeat is happy.

There is no burning fire like passion;
There is no losing throw like one's hatred;
There is no piercing pain like this body;
There is no happiness higher than rest.

Hunger is the worst of diseases and
The body the greatest of pains; if one
Knows this truly, then that is Nirvana.

Health is the greatest of possible gifts,
And contentedness the best of riches;
Trust is the best of all relationships,
And Nirvana the highest happiness.

He who tastes the sweetness of solitude
And tranquility, he is free from fear
And also free from sin, while he savors
The sweetness of drinking within the law.

He who walks in the company of fools
Suffers a long way; company with fools,
As with enemies, is always painful;
Walking in company with the wise is
A true pleasure, like meeting with kinsfolk.

Therefore, one ought to follow the wise and
The intelligent, the learned and
The much enduring, the dutiful and
The elect; one ought to follow a good
And wise man, as the moon follows the stars.

He who gives himself to vanity, and
Does not give himself to meditation,
Forgetting the real aim of life, grasping
At pleasure, will in time envy him who
Exerted himself in meditation.

He who possesses both intelligence
And virtue, who is just, speaks truth, and does
His own business, him the world will hold dear.

Let a man leave anger, let him forsake
Pride, and let him overcome all bondage!
No sufferings befall him who is not
Attached to name and form, who owns nothing.

He who holds back rising anger like a
Rolling chariot is a real driver;
Other people are but holding the reins.

Let a man overcome anger by love,
Let him overcome the evil by good;
And let him overcome the greedy by
Liberality, the liar by truth!

Those who are ever watchful, who study
Day and night, and strive after Nirvana,
Their passions will surely come to an end.

This is an old saying, 'They blame him who
Sits silent, they blame him who speaks too much,
They also blame him who says but little;
There is no one on earth who is not blamed.'

There never was, there never will be, nor
Is there now, anyone who is always
Blamed, or anyone who is always praised.

Beware bodily anger, and control
Your body! Leave the sins of the body,
And then practice virtue with your body!

Beware of the anger of the tongue, and
Control your tongue! Leave the sins of the tongue,
And then practice firm virtue with your tongue!

Beware of the anger of the mind, and
Control your mind! Leave the sins of the mind,
And then practice firm virtue with your mind!

And the wise who control their body, and
Who control their tongue, the wise who control
Their mind, they are certainly well controlled.

Let a wise man blow off impurities
Of his self, just as a smith blows off the
Impurities of silver – one by one,
Little by little, and from time to time.

As the impurity which springs from the
Iron, when it springs from it, destroys it;
Thus do a transgressor's own works lead him.

The mantra's taint is non-repetition;

The taint of houses is in disrepair;
The taint of the body is by its sloth;
The taint of a watchman is thoughtlessness.

But there is a taint worse than all others —
Ignorance is truly the greatest taint.
Mendicants, throw off that taint! Be taintless!

Life is easy to live for any man
Who is without shame, as a crow hero,
A mischief-maker, an insulting, bold,
And more — a thoroughly wretched fellow.

Life is hard to live for a modest man,
Who always looks for what is truly pure,
Who is disinterested, and quiet,
Who is spotless, and is intelligent.

He who destroys life, who dares speak untruth,
Who in this world takes what is not given
To him, who goes to another man's wife;
And the man who gives himself to drinking
Intoxicating liquors, such a one,
Even in this world, digs up his own root.

O man, know this, that the unrestrained are
In a bad state; take care that greediness
And vice do not bring you to a long grief!

There is no fire like passion, there is
No shark like hatred, there is no snare like
Folly, and there is no torrent like greed.

Fault in others is easily perceived,
But that of oneself is difficult to

Perceive; a man winnows his neighbor's faults
Like chaff, but his own fault he would hide, as
A cheat hides the bad die from the gambler.

If one looks after the faults of others,
Is always inclined to be offended,
His own passions will have increase, and he
Is far from the destruction of passions.

There is no path through the air, a man is
Not a Samana by his outward acts.
The world delights in vanity, but the
Awakened, they are free from vanity.

There is no path through the air, a man is
Not a Samana by his outward acts.
No creatures remain alive forever;
But the awakened are never shaken.

A man is not just if he carries a
Matter by violence; no, and yet he who
Distinguishes both right and wrong, who is
Learned and leads others, not by violence,
But by law and equity, and who is
Guarded by the law and intelligent,
It is such a man that we may call just.

A man is not learned because he talks
A great deal; he who is patient, and free
From hatred and fear, he is called learned.

A man is not a supporter of law
Because he talks much; even if a man
Has learnt but a little, yet sees the law
Bodily, he is a supporter of

The law, a man who never neglects it.

A man is not an elder just because
The hair on his head is grey; his age may
Be ripe, yet still he is called 'old-in-vain.'

The one in whom there is truth, virtue, love,
Restraint, moderation, who is wise and
Free from impurity, is an elder.

An envious, greedy, dishonest man
Can never become respectable by
Means of a great deal of talking only,
Or by the beauty of his complexion.

And he in whom all this is destroyed, and
Taken out with the very root, he, when
Freed from hatred, is called respectable.

Not by tonsure does the undisciplined
Who speaks falsehood become a quiet man;
Can a man be a quiet man who is
Still held captive by desire and greed?

He who can always quiet the evil,
Whether small or large, is a quiet man,
Because he has quieted all evil.

A man is not a mendicant simply
Because he asks others for alms; he who
Adopts the whole law is a monk and a
Mendicant, and not he who only begs.

He who is above good and evil, who
Is chaste, who with knowledge passes through the

World, he indeed is called a mendicant.

A man is not a Muni because he
Observes silence, if he is foolish and
Ignorant; but the wise who, taking the
Balance, chooses good and avoids evil,
He is a Muni thereby; in this world
He who weighs both sides is called a Muni.

And a man is not an elect because
He does injury to living creatures;
Because he has pity on all living
Creatures, therefore is a man called elect.

Not only by discipline and by vows,
Not only by immense learning, not by
Entering into a trance, and not by
Sleeping alone, do I earn the pure joy
Of release, which none of the world can know.
Monk, be not confident as long as you
Have not attained desire extinction.

The best of ways is that of the eightfold;
The best of truths is that of the four words;
The best of virtues, lack of attachment;
The best of men, he who has eyes to see.

This is the way, as there is no other
That will purify the intelligence.
All else is the deceit of the tempter.

If you go on this way, you will make an
End of pain! The way was preached by me, when
I understood the removal of thorns.

And you yourself must make the great effort,
For all the Buddhas are only preachers.
The thoughtful who enter the way are freed
From the bondage of the tempter, Mara.

He who does not rouse himself when it is
Time for him to rise, who, though young and strong,
Is full of sloth, whose will and thought are weak,
Such a lazy and idle person will
Never find the way to knowledge and truth.

Through zeal knowledge is gotten, through its lack,
Knowledge is lost; let a man who knows this
Double path of gain and loss place himself
Accordingly so that knowledge may grow.

Cut out the love of self, like an autumn
Lotus, with your hand! Cherish the road of
Peace. Nirvana has been shown by Buddha.

'Here I shall dwell in the rain, here in the
Winter and summer,' in this way a fool
Meditates, and does not think of his death.

Death comes and carries off that man, praised for
His children and flocks, his mind distracted,
As a flood carries a sleeping village.

Sons are no help, nor a father, nor are
Relations; there is no help from any
Kinsfolk for anyone whom death has seized.

A wise and good man who knows the meaning
Of this, should clear the way to Nirvana.

If by leaving a small pleasure one sees
A great pleasure, then let a wise person
Leave the small pleasure, and look to the great.

The one who, by causing pain to others,
Wishes to obtain pleasure for himself,
He, entangled in the bonds of hatred,
Will never be free from that same hatred.

What ought to be done is just neglected,
And what ought not to be done is still done;
The desires of the unruly and
Thoughtless people are always increasing.

Disciples of Gotama are always
Well awake, and their thoughts during the day
And the night are always set on Buddha.

Disciples of Gotama are always
Well awake, and their thoughts during the day
And the night are always set on the law.

Disciples of Gotama are always
Well awake, and their thoughts during the day
And the night are always set on the church.

Disciples of Gotama are always
Well awake, and their thoughts during the day
And night are always set on their body.

Disciples of Gotama are always
Well awake, and their mind during the day
And night always delights in compassion.

Disciples of Gotama are always

Well awake, and their mind during day and
Night always delights in meditation.

It is hard to leave the world as a monk,
It is hard to enjoy the world also;
Hard is the monastery, painful are
The houses; painful it is to dwell with
Equals — to share everything in common —
And the itinerant mendicant is
Beset with pain. Therefore let no man be
An itinerant mendicant and then
He will not be so beset with that pain.

Whatever place a faithful, virtuous,
Celebrated, and wealthy man chooses,
In that place, such a man is respected.

Good people shine from afar, just like the
Snowy mountains; bad people are not seen,
And they are like arrows shot in the night.

He who says what is not, he is evil;
He also who, having done a thing, says
I have not done it. After death both are
Equal — men with evil in the next world.

Better it would be to swallow heated
Iron balls, like flaring fire, than that
A horrible unrestrained fellow should
Live off of the charity of the land.

Acts carelessly performed, a broken vow,
And hesitating obedience to
Discipline, all this brings no great reward.

If anything is to be done, let a
Person then do it, let him attack it
Vigorously! A careless pilgrim just
Scatters the dust of passions more widely.

Like a well-guarded frontier fort, with its
Defenses within and without, so let
A man guard himself. Not a moment should
Escape, for they who allow the right time
To pass, they will suffer eternal pain.

They who are ashamed of what they ought not
To be ashamed of, and are not ashamed
Of what they ought to be ashamed, such men,
Embracing false doctrines walk the foul path.

And they who fear when they ought not to fear,
And fear not when they ought to fear, such men,
Embracing false doctrines walk the foul path.

And they who forbid when there is nothing
To be forbidden, and forbid not when
There are things to be forbidden, such men,
Embracing false doctrines walk the foul path.

Silently shall I endure abuse as
The elephant in battle endures the
Bow's arrow: for the world is ill-natured.

Mules are good, if tamed, and noble horses,
And also the elephants with large tusks;
But he who tames himself is better still.

For with these animals does no man reach
The untrodden country – reach Nirvana,

Where a tamed man will go upon a tamed
Animal — that is, on his well-tamed self.

If a man becomes fat — a great eater,
If he is sleepy and rolls around, that
Fool, like a hog fed on wash, he is trapped.

My mind, it went formerly wandering
About as it liked, as it listed, as
It pleased; but I shall now rein my mind in
Thoroughly, as the rider who holds the
Hook holds in the furious elephant.

Be not thoughtless, but also watch your thoughts!
And draw yourself out of the evil way,
As if an elephant sunk in the mud.

If a man find a prudent companion
Who walks with him, is wise, lives soberly,
He may walk with that one, overcoming
All dangers, happy, but considerate.

If a man find no prudent companion
Who walks with him, is wise, lives soberly,
Let him walk alone, just as a king who
Has left his conquered country far behind,
And like an elephant in the forest.

If an occasion arises, friends are
Pleasant; enjoyment is also pleasant,
Whatever be the cause; a good work is
Also pleasant in the hour of death;
The giving up of all grief is pleasant.

Pleasant in the world is the state of a

Mother, pleasant the state of a father,
Pleasant is the state of an ascetic,
And pleasant also the state of a priest.

Pleasant is virtue lasting to old age,
Pleasant is a faith when firmly rooted;
Pleasant is intelligence attainment,
And pleasant is the avoiding of wrongs.

The thirst of a thoughtless man grows like a
Creeper; he runs from life to life, much like
A monkey seeking fruit in the forest.

And whoever this fierce thirst overcomes,
Full of its poison, in this world, then his
Sufferings increase like abounding grass.

He who overcomes this fierce thirst, which is
Difficult to be conquered in this world,
All the world's sufferings fall off from him,
Just like water-drops from a lotus leaf.

As a tree, even though it has been cut
Down, is firm so long as its root is safe,
And grows again, thus, unless the feeders
Of thirst are completely destroyed, the pain
Of life will return again and again.

He whose thirst running towards pleasure is
Exceedingly strong, the waves will carry
Away that misguided man – desires
Which are set on passion carry him off.

The channels run everywhere, the creeper
Sprouting; if you see the creeper springing

Up, then cut its root by means of knowledge.

He who having got rid of the forest
Gives himself over to forest-life, and
Who, removed from the forest, runs to it,
Look at that man! Free, he runs to bondage.

If a man is tossed about by doubts, full
Of strong passions, and yearning only for
What is delightful, his thirst will grow more
And he will indeed make his fetters strong.

If a man delights in quieting doubts,
And, always reflecting, dwells on what is
Not delightful, he surely will remove,
He will cut the fetter of the tempter.

He who has reached the consummation, who
Does not tremble, who is without thirst and
Without sin, he has broken all the thorns
Of life: this one will be his last body.

He who is without thirst and without cares,
Understands words and interpretations,
Who knows the order of letters, he has
His last body, he is called the great sage.

'I have conquered all, I know all, in all
Conditions of life I am free from taint;
Through the destruction of thirst I am free;
And having learnt myself, whom shall I teach?'

The fields are damaged by weeds, mankind is
Damaged by unreason: therefore a gift
Bestowed on the reasoned brings great reward.

The fields are damaged by weeds, mankind is
Damaged by hatred: therefore any gift
To those who do not hate brings great reward.

The fields are damaged by weeds, mankind is
Damaged by vanity: therefore a gift
To those vanity-free brings great reward.

The fields are damaged by weeds, mankind is
Damaged by lust: therefore a gift bestowed
Upon those free from lust brings great reward.

Restraint in the eye is good, and good is
Restraint in the ear, in the nose restraint
Is good, and good is restraint in the tongue.

In the body restraint is good, good is
Restraint in speech, in thought restraint is good,
Good is restraint in all things. A monk who
Is restrained in all things is freed from pain.

He who controls his hand, he who controls
His feet, he who controls his speech, he who
Is well controlled, who delights inwardly,
Who is collected, is solitary
And content in that, him they call a monk.

The monk who has control over his mouth,
Who speaks wisely and calmly, who teaches
The meaning and the law, his word is sweet.

He who never identifies himself
With name and form, and does not grieve over
What is no more, he indeed is a monk.

The monk who acts with kindness, who is calm
In the doctrine of the Awakened, will
Reach the quiet place, the cessation of
Natural desires, and happiness.

Without knowledge there's no meditation,
Without meditation there's no knowledge:
He who has knowledge and meditation
Such a one is nearer to Nirvana.

As soon as anyone has considered
The origin and destruction of the
Elements of the body, he finds joy
Which belongs to those who know Nirvana.

Rouse yourself by yourself, and examine
Yourself by yourself, thus self-protected
And attentive will you live happily.

For self is the lord of self, self is the
Refuge of self, and therefore curb yourself
Just as the merchant will curb a good horse.

Stop the stream valiantly, drive away
The desires, O Brahmana! When you
Have understood the end of all that was
Made, you will understand that which was not.

The sun shines by day, the moon shines by night,
The warrior is bright in his armor,
The Brahmana, bright in meditation;
But the Awakened is bright day and night.

No one should attack a Brahmana, but

No Brahmana attacked should let himself
Fly at his aggressor! Woe to him who
Strikes, more woe to him who retaliates!

Him I call indeed a Brahmana who
Does not offend by body, word, or thought,
And is controlled on each of these three points.

A man does not become a Brahmana
By platted hair, by family, or by
Birth; in whom there is truth and righteousness,
He is blessed, he is a Brahmana.

What is the use of platted hair, O fool!
What of the raiment of goat-skins? Within
You there is greed, but the outside, you clean.

Him I call indeed a Brahmana who
Has cut all fetters, who never trembles,
Who is independent and unshackled.

Him I call indeed a Brahmana who,
Though he has committed no offence, bears
Reproach, bonds, and stripes, who has endurance
For his force, and strength, too, for his army.

Him I call indeed a Brahmana who
Is free from anger, who is dutiful,
Virtuous, without appetite, who is
Subdued, and has received his last body.

Him I call indeed a Brahmana who
Does not cling to any pleasures, just like
Water on a lotus leaf, or like a
Mustard seed on the point of a needle.

Him I call indeed a Brahmana who,
Even here, knows his suffering's end, has
Put down his burden, and is unshackled.

Him I call indeed a Brahmana whose
Knowledge is deep, who possesses wisdom,
Who knows the correct way and the wrong way
And who has then attained the highest end.

Him I call indeed a Brahmana who
Finds no fault with other beings, whether
Weak or strong, and does not kill, nor cause it.

Him I call indeed a Brahmana who
Is tolerant with the intolerant,
Mild with all the fault-finders, and also
Free from passion among the passionate.

Him I call indeed a Brahmana from
Whom anger and hatred, pride and envy
Fall like a mustard seed from a needle.

Him I call indeed a Brahmana who
Utters true speech, instructive and free from
Harshness, so that he will offend no one.

Him I call indeed a Brahmana who
Will take nothing in the world that is not
Given him — long, short, small, large, good, or bad.

Him I call indeed a Brahmana who
Fosters no desires for this world or
For the next, and has no inclinations.

Him I call indeed a Brahmana who
In this world is above good and evil,
Above the bondage of both, free from grief
From sin, and also from impurity.

Him I call indeed a Brahmana who
Is bright like the moon, serene, undisturbed,
Pure, and in whom all tempest is extinct.

Him I call indeed a Brahmana who
Has traversed this miry road; the world and
Its vanity, who has gone through, and reached
The other shore, is thoughtful, guileless, free
From doubts, free from attachment, and content.

Him I call indeed a Brahmana who
Leaving all desires, travels without
A home, in whom all longing is extinct.

Him I call indeed a Brahmana who,
Leaving longings, travels without a home,
In whom all covetousness is extinct.

Him I call indeed a Brahmana who,
After leaving all bondage to men, has
Risen above all bondage to the gods,
And is free from all and every bondage.

Him I call indeed a Brahmana who
Has left what gives pleasure and what gives pain,
Who is cold, and free from all worldly germs,
The hero who has conquered all the worlds.

Him I call indeed a Brahmana who
Knows the destruction and the return of

Beings everywhere, is free from bondage,
Welfaring, and awakened as Buddha.

Him I call indeed a Brahmana whose
Path the gods know not, nor spirits, nor men,
With passions extinct, who is an elder.

Him I call indeed a Brahmana who
Calls nothing his own, no matter if it
Is before, behind, or between, who is
Poor, and is free from the love of the world.

Him I call indeed a Brahmana, the
Manly, the noble, the hero, the sage,
The great conqueror, the impassible,
The much accomplished, and the Awakened.

The Prophet
The Teachings of Jesus Christ

Jesus Christ is, put quite simply, the most influential figure in the Western world. Due to a lack of historical records from his time and differing depictions in the gospels, there is some disagreement among biblical scholars about who exactly he was. There is, thankfully, less uncertainty about what he believed.

Much of what Christ says, as recorded in the King James Version of the Bible and the gospel of Thomas, concern piety towards God and belief in him as a means of salvation. However, even though he ends many parables by interpreting them in a manner relating to matters of piety, the parables at face value tend to concern ethics. I have taken advantage of this double meaning as a reason to include those parables here, without the reinterpretations specific to Christianity.

Since most of what follows will be familiar to readers, it is interesting to see how the ideas of Christ compare with those of the other authors. There are clear parallels between him, Buddha, and Marcus Aurelius. All three set fairly high ethical standards compared to the practical expectations of Confucius. Whereas Buddha's words are especially concerned with ignorance and desires, Christ's are more adamant on the topic of hypocrisy. His most strident rhetoric attacks those who do not suit their words to their actions.

It is also noticeable that Christ employs analogies in a way similar to Buddha – frequently using everyday comparisons that everyone in the society would be able to grasp and remember. This is likely due to the similarity in their target audience. They both spoke to large groups of individuals with diverse backgrounds. By contrast, Confucius directed his teachings to a highly educated class, and so used historical examples, while Marcus Aurelius had himself as his sole audience, and most often used individuals that he admired or examples he had personally observed. Patanjali is the most obscure, because he directed his comments to a highly specialized group of yogis who employed a very particular vocabulary to describe the important ideas in their art.

The Teachings of Jesus Christ
(excerpts)

I shall give you what no man's eye has seen
What no ear has heard, what no hand has touched
What has never occurred to human minds.

The Pharisees and the scribes have taken
The keys of knowledge and have hidden them.
They themselves have not entered, nor have they
Allowed to enter those who have wished to.

The grapes are not harvested from the thorns,
Nor are the figs gathered from the thistles.
A good man brings forth good from his storehouse;
Evil men bring forth evil things from theirs.
It is by their fruits that you should know men.

Blessed are the poor, for heaven is theirs.
Bless'd are the mourning, for comfort is theirs.
Blessed are they who, for righteousness sake
Do hunger and thirst, for they shall be filled.
Bless'd are the pure in heart, for truth is theirs.
Blessed are the meek, for the earth is theirs.
Bless'd are the lovers and makers of peace
For they shall be called the children of God.
And blessed are you when men revile you
And persecute you for righteousness sake.
Rejoice, be glad, for great is your reward
In heaven and on earth, for before you

The prophets, too, were so persecuted.
Remember, you are the salt of the earth —
And yet, if the salt has lost its savor,
It is thenceforth not good for anything.
Remember, you are the light of the world —
Let your light shine before men through good works.

You have heard it was said by those of old
You shall not kill, and whosoever kills
Shall then be in danger of the judgment,
But I say to you that whosoever
Is angry with his brother without cause,
He shall then be in danger of judgment.

Be quick to agree with adversaries
While you can still be reconciled with them,
Lest at any time the adversaries
Deliver you to a judge, and prison.

You have heard it was said by those of old
That you shall not commit adultery,
But I say to you that whosoever
Looks on a woman to lust after her
Has committed adultery at heart.

You have heard it was said by those of old
That you hall not forswear yourself, but shall
Perform in strict accordance with your oaths,
But I say to you, do not swear at all,
Neither by heaven, nor by the earth, nor
By Jerusalem. Neither should you swear
By a head you cannot change a hair on.
Let your communication be: yes; no.

You have heard it was said by those of old

An eye for an eye; a tooth for a tooth,
But I say to you, to whosoever
Strikes you on your right cheek, show him your left.
If any man would sue you at the law,
Taking your coat, let him have your cloak, too.
And whosoever shall compel you to
Go with him a mile, go with him two miles.
Give to him who asks, and from the one who
Would borrow from you, do not turn away.

You have heard it was said by those of old
You should love your neighbor and hate your foe,
But I say to you that instead, you should
Love your enemies, bless them that curse you,
Do good to all those that hate you, and pray
For those who use you, and persecute you.
For even the least love those who love them —
And if you salute your brethren only,
What is it you do more than others do?

And when you do your alms, do not sound a
Trumpet before you, as the hypocrites
Do in the synagogues and in the streets,
That they may have glory of men. Truly,
I say unto you, they have their reward.
But when you do your alms, do not let your
Left hand know what your right hand is doing.

Do not judge as you would not be judged, for
With what judgment you judge, you shall be judged.
And with whatever measure you mete out,
That one shall be measured to you again.
And why do you behold the mote that is
In your brother's eye, and yet you do not
Consider the beam that is in your own?

Or how will you then say to your brother,
"Let me pull out the mote out of your eye"
While, behold, a beam is in your own eye?
You hypocrite, first cast out the beam from
Your own eye, and then you will see clearly
To cast the mote out of your brother's eye.

Give not that which is holy unto dogs,
Neither cast your pearls before swine, lest they
Trample them under their feet, and rend you.

Ask, and it shall be given to you. Seek,
And you shall find. Knock, it shall be opened.
For what man is there of you whom if his
Son asks for bread, will then give him a stone?
Or if he asks a fish, gives a serpent?

Enter in at the strait gate, for truly
Wide is the gate and broad is the way that
Leads to destruction, as many go thus.
For strait is the gate and narrow the way
Which leads to life, and few there that find it.

Beware of false prophets, which come to you
In sheep's clothing, but are inwardly wolves.
You will know them by their fruits. For do men
Gather grapes of thorns, or figs of thistles?
Even so, every good tree brings forth
Good fruit, but corrupt trees bring evil fruit.
A good tree cannot bring forth evil fruit,
Neither can a corrupt tree bring good fruit.
Every tree that brings not forth good fruit
Is hewn down, and cast into the fire.

Whosoever hears these sayings of mine

And does them, I will liken him unto
A wise man, which built his house on a rock:
And the rain descended, and the floods came,
And the winds blew, and beat upon that house,
And it fell not, founded upon a rock.
And each one who hears these sayings of mine,
And does them not, shall be likened unto
A foolish man, who built his house on sand:
And the rain descended, and the floods came,
And the winds blew, and beat upon that house,
And it fell, and great was the fall of it.

Every kingdom divided against
Itself is thus brought to desolation,
And every city or house that is
Divided against itself shall not stand.

A sower went forth to sow. When he sowed,
Some seeds fell by the wayside, and the fowls
Came and devoured them up. Some fell on
Stony places, where they had not much earth,
And forthwith they sprung up because they had
No deepness of earth. And when the sun rose
They were scorched, and because they had no root,
They withered away. And some fell among
Thorns, and those same thorns sprung up and choked them.
But others fell into good ground, and they
Brought forth fruit – some a hundredfold, some less.

Not that which goes into the mouth defiles
A man, but that which comes out of the mouth.
Do you not understand, that whatever
Enters in at the mouth goes into the
Belly, and is cast out into the draught?
But those things which proceed out of the mouth

Come forth from the heart, and can defile man.

When it is evening you say it will
Be fair weather because the sky is red.
And in the morning, that it will be foul
Weather today, because the sky is red
And lowering. O you hypocrites, you
Can discern the face of the sky, but can
You not then discern the signs of the times?
A wicked generation seeks a sign.

If a man has a hundred sheep, and one
Of them has gone astray, does he not leave
The ninety-nine, go into the mountains,
And seek after that which is gone astray?
And if he finds it, I say to you that
He rejoices more in that sheep than in
The ninety-nine which did not go astray.

If your brother trespasses against you,
Tell him this between you and him alone.
If he hears you, you have gained your brother.
If he will not hear you, then take with you
One or two more, that in the mouth of two
Or three witnesses each word is certain.

If you will enter into life, keep these
Commandments: You shall do no murder, you
Shall not commit adultery, you shall
Not steal, and you shall not bear false witness.
Honor your father and your mother, and
Love your neighbor, just as you love yourself.

You know that the princes of the Gentiles
Exercise dominion over them, and

The great impose authority on them.
But it shall not be so among you, and
Whosoever will be great among you,
Let him be your minister, and who would
Be chief among you, let be your servant.
Even as the son of man came not to
Be ministered to, but to minister,
To give his life as ransom for many.

Scribes and Pharisees sit in the seat
Of Moses. Therefore, all they bid you to
Observe, that observe and do, but do not
After their works, for they say and do not.
For they bind heavy burdens and grievous
To be borne, and lay them on men's shoulders,
But they themselves will not move a finger.
But all their works they do for to be seen
Of men: they make broad their phylacteries,
And enlarge the borders of their garments,
And love the uppermost rooms at feasts, and
Also the chief seats in the synagogues.
They love, too, the greetings in the markets
And to be called by men, Rabbi, Rabbi.

Woe to you, scribes, Pharisees, hypocrites!
For you devour widows' houses and
But for a pretense you make long prayer.
Woe to you, scribes, Pharisees, hypocrites!
For you compass sea and land to make one
Proselyte, and when he is made, you make
Him twofold more the child of hell than you.
Woe to you, blind guides, who say whoever
Shall swear by the temple, it is nothing,
But that whosoever shall swear by the
Gold of the temple, he is a debtor!

You fools and blind – for which is the greater:
The gold, or temple that sanctifies it?
Woe to you, scribes, Pharisees, hypocrites!
For you pay tithe of mint and anise and
Cummin, and omitted the weightier
Matters of the law, judgment, mercy, and
Faith. These ought you to have done, and not leave
The other undone. You blind guides which strain
At a gnat, and yet swallow a camel.
Woe to you, scribes, Pharisees, hypocrites!
For you make clean the outside of the cup
And of the platter, and yet within them
They are full of extortion and excess.
You, blind Pharisee, cleanse first that which is
Within the cup and platter, and after
The outside of them may be cleaned also.
Woe to you, scribes, Pharisees, hypocrites!
For you are like the whited sepulchres
Which indeed appear beautiful outward,
But within are full of dead men's bones, and
Of all uncleanness. Thus you also seem
Outwardly righteous, but within are full
Of hypocrisy and iniquity.

Ten virgins took lamps to meet the bridegroom –
Five of them were wise, and five were foolish.
The foolish took their lamps, and took no oil,
But the wise took oil vessels with their lamps.
While the bridegroom tarried, they all slumbered.
And at midnight, a cry rang out: "Behold,
The bridegroom comes, go you out to meet him."
Then all the virgins rose and trimmed their lamps.
And the foolish said to the wise, "Give us
Some of your oil, for our lamps have gone out."
But the wise answered, 'No, for there will not

Be enough for us and you. Go instead
To those that sell it, and buy for yourselves."
And while they went to buy, the bridegroom came
And they who were ready went in with him
To the marriage, and the door was then shut.

A man traveling to a far country
Called his servants to distribute his goods.
To one he gave five talents, to the next
Two, and to another one – to each man
According to his ability, and
Thereafter straightaway took his journey.
He who received the five talents went and
Traded with the same, and made them five more.
Likewise, he who received two, gained two more.
But he that had received one went and dug
In the earth, and he hid his lord's money.
And after a long time, the lord returned,
And so he who had received five talents,
And brought five more talents, said, "Lord, you gave
To me five talents, and behold, I gained
Beside them five talents more." His lord said
To him, "Well done, good and faithful servant.
You have been faithful over a few things,
I will make you ruler over many."
He that received two talents also came
And said, "Lord, you gave to me two talents.
Behold, I have gained two other talents."
His lord said to him, "Well done, good, faithful
Servant. Being true over a few things,
I will make you ruler over many."
Then he who had received the one talent
Came and said, "Lord, I knew that you are a
Hard man, reaping where you have not sown, and
Gathering where you have not strawed, and I

Was afraid, and went and hid your talent
In the earth – and here, you have what is yours."
His lord answered, "You wicked and slothful
Servant. You knew I reaped where I sowed not,
And that I gather where I have not strawed.
You ought therefore to have put my money
To exchangers, and on my return I
Should have received my own with usury.
Give, then, the talent to he who has ten,
For to everyone who has, shall be
Given, and he shall have abundance, but
From he that has not, all shall be taken –
Even that which he has shall be taken.

Then the king shall say to those on his right:
"Inherit the kingdom prepared for you
For I was hungered, and you gave me meat;
For I was thirsty, and you gave me drink;
I was a stranger, and you took me in;
Naked, you clothed me; sick, you visited;
I was in prison, and you came to me."
Then shall the righteous answer him, saying,
"Lord, when did we see you as hungered, and
Fed you, or thirsty, and gave to you drink?
When did we see you as a stranger and
Then take you in? Or naked, and clothed you?
When did we see you sick or in prison?"
And the king shall answer and say to them:
"Truly I say to you, inasmuch as
You have done it to the least of these my
Brethren, you have done it also to me."

Put up your sword into its place, for all
Who take the sword shall perish by the sword.

There was a certain creditor which had
Two debtors: the one owed five hundred pence,
And the other fifty. And when they had
Nothing to pay, he frankly forgave both.
Tell me then, which of them will love him most?

A man went down from Jerusalem to
Jericho, and fell among thieves, which stripped
Him of his raiment, and wounded him, and
When they departed, they left him half dead.
By chance there came down a priest that way, who
Saw him, and passed by on the other side.
Likewise a Levite, reaching that place, looked
On him, and passed by on the other side.
But a Samaritan, as he journeyed,
Came where he was, and when he say him, he
Had compassion on him, and went to him,
And bound up his wounds, pouring in oil and
Wine, and set him on his own beast, and brought
The man to an inn, and took care of him.
And on the morrow, when he departed,
He took out two pence, gave them to the host,
And said unto him, "Take care of him, and
Whatever you spend more, I will repay."
Which now of these three do you think was a
Neighbor to he who fell among the thieves?

Man, who made me a judge or divider
Over you? Take heed, then, and beware of
Covetousness. For a man's life consists
Not in the abundance of things he owns.

Who, then, is that faithful and wise steward
Whom his lord shall make ruler over his
Household, to give them due portion of meat?

Blessed is that servant, whom his lord when
He comes shall find so doing. Of a truth,
I say unto you that he will make him
Ruler over all that he has. But if
That servant should say in his heart, my lord
Delays his coming, and shall begin to
Beat the menservants and the maidens and
To eat and to drink and to be drunken,
The lord of that servant will return on
A day his servant does not expect and
At an hour when he is not aware,
And will then cut the servant asunder.

When you are bidden of any man to
A wedding, do not take the highest place
In case a more honorable man comes
And he that bade you and he who has come
Say to you, "Give this man place," and with shame
You must move to take the lowest of seats.
But when you are bidden, go and sit down
In the lowest, so when he that bade you
Comes to you, he may say unto you, "Friend,
Go up higher." Then you shall have worship
In the presence of them that sit at meat.
For who exalts himself shall be abased.
He that is humble shall be exalted.

Who then, intending to build a tower,
Does not sit down first, determine the cost,
And see if he has enough to finish?
In case, after he laid the foundation,
And is unable to finish it, all
That see it begin to mock him, saying,
"He began to build, and could not finish."
Or what king, going to make war against

Another king, does not sit down first and
Consider whether he is able with
Ten thousand to oppose twenty thousand?
Or else, while the other is still a great
Way off, he sends an ambassador and
Thereby discovers conditions for peace.

A certain man had two sons, and of them
The younger said to his father, "Father,
Give me the portion of goods that falls to
Me," and he divided to them his wealth.
And not many days after, the younger
Son gathered all together, and took his
Journey into a far country, and there
Wasted his substance in riotous life.
And when he had spent all, there arose a
Mighty famine in that land, so that then
He began to be in want. And he went
And joined himself to a citizen of
That country, and was sent to feed the swine.
And he would gladly have filled his belly
With the husks the swine ate, and none gave him.
When he at last came to himself, he said,
"How many servants of my father's have
Bread enough and to spare, and I hunger!
I will arise and go to my father
And will say to him, Father, I have sinned
Against heaven and before you, and am
No longer worthy to be called your son.
Make me as one of your hired servants."
And he arose and came to his father.
But when he was as yet a great way off,
His father saw him, and had compassion,
And ran, and fell on his neck, and kissed him.
The son said to him, "Father, I have sinned

Against heaven and before you, and am
No longer worthy to be called your son."
And yet the father said to his servants,
"Bring forth the best robe, and put it on him.
Put a ring on his hand, shoes on his feet,
And bring here the fatted calf, and kill it,
And let us eat, and be merry, for this
My son was dead, and is alive again.
He was lost, and is found." And they did so.
Now the elder son was in the field and
As he came to the house, he heard music
And dancing. And he called to one servant
And asked what these things meant, and he was told:
"Your brother has come, and your father has
Killed the fatted calf, for his safe return."
And the elder brother became angry
And would not go in, therefore his father
Came out to him, and entreated with him.
And he, answering, said to his father,
"These many years I have served you, have not
At any time transgressed your commandments,
But you have never given me a kid
So that I might make merry with my friends.
Yet as soon as your son has come, who has
Devoured your living with the harlots,
You have killed for his sake the fatted calf."
And his father said to him, "Son, you are
Ever with me, and all I have is yours.
It was right that we should make merry and
Be glad, for your brother was dead, and is
Alive again. He was lost, and is found."

He that is faithful in that which is least
Is also faithful in much. He that is
Unjust in the least, also is in much.

If therefore you have not been faithful in
The unrighteous mammon, who will commit
To your trust true riches. If you have not
Been faithful in that which is another's,
Then who shall give you that which is your own?

If your brother trespasses against you,
Rebuke him. If he repents, forgive him.

Judge not according to the appearance,
But rather judge by a righteous judgment.

Let him who seeks not cease until he finds
And when he finds, he will become troubled
And, astonished, he will rule over all.

If they say the kingdom is in the sky,
Then the birds of the sky will precede you.
If they say to you it is in the sea,
Then the fish of the sea will precede you.
When you know yourselves, you will be known,
And you will realize that it is you
Who are the sons of the living father.
Not knowing, you will dwell in poverty,
And it is you who are that poverty.

First recognize that which is in your sight
And that which is hidden will become plain.

Tell no lies, and do not do what you hate,
For your resentment will be uncovered.

The kingdom is like a wise fisherman
Who cast his net into the sea and drew
His net up from the sea full of small fish

And among them he found a fine large fish
Which he then chose without difficulty
Returning the small fish back to the sea.

Where the beginning is, there the end is.
He who takes his place in the beginning
He will know the end, and will not face death.

I took my place in the midst of the world.
Finding all of them intoxicated,
I found none of them thirsty, and my soul
Became afflicted for the sons of men
Because their hearts are blind, and they lack sight.
For empty did they come into the world,
And empty, too, they seek to leave the world.
But for now, they are intoxicated.
When they shake off their wine, they will repent.

No prophet is loved in his own village,
Nor does a physician cure those he knows.

A city built on top of a high hill
Can neither easily fall, nor be hid.

Be not concerned from morning till evening
About what you eat, or what you will wear.

Whoever finds the interpretation
Of these words will not experience death.

The Spiritual Man
The Yoga Sutras of Patanjali

Both Buddha and Marcus Aurelius emphasize the importance of meditation and contemplation in the way of life they prescribe. Patanjali's *Yoga Sutras* is the most famous text regarding the practice of yogic meditation and its associated ethics. Of the five main authors included in this collection, Patanjali is the most obscure, with probable date for his life being somewhere in the 2nd century B.C. Otherwise, he is known exclusively by these sutras, and a few other works attributed to him.

Unfortunately, Patanjali's personal obscurity is matched by the unclear meaning of much of his work. The reason for this is not imprecision on his part, but rather the opposite. The terms he used are highly technical, and the reader is expected to be already familiar with them. Worse, many of the terms do not occur in any other extant work. The result is that translations can be wildly varying, and largely depend on the philosophical bias of the translator.

For the version included here, I have preferred simplicity, aiming for translations that would be the most easily grasped by the casual reader. It is necessary, though, to highlight the fact that while the text as rendered here provides a good overview of Patanjali's ideas, it lacks an ocean's worth of depth. As it is, this version is already quite dense and will take some effort to get through. People can, and have, spent decades parsing the original text out and interpreting it.

In many ways, the *Yoga Sutras* is a logical culmination of the flow of ideas already established throughout this book. It sets forth in short form many of the issue already brought up by the other authors – attachment, desire, and ignorance. It outlines the solutions to the pains of the world, promising definite benefits in exchange for practice and discipline.

The Yoga Sutras of Patanjali
(complete)

Yoga is control over consciousness
So that we can unify our nature
Which is now divided between two realms.
Otherwise we are as slaves to our thoughts.

Our base mind states appears in five-fold streams:
Right and Wrong Knowledge, Fancy, Memory,
Sleep; each can be painful or not painful.
Right knowledge is perception, inference,
And learning from other's experience.
Wrong knowledge is assumption, illusion,
And all unfounded beliefs or notions.
Fancy is unknowable creation.
Sleep is the purging of the mind's concerns.
Memory is impression retention.

These five thought streams are controlled by practice.
Practice is the effort to be steady
And non-attachment well-grounds all practice,
As does continuation of practice
With focus, over a long period.
Consciousness mastery is signified
By desirelessness and indifference
And meditation leads to mastery.

Object-oriented meditation
Starts with reasoning, discrimination,
Then proceeds through joy of understanding
And the knowledge of existence itself.
Another meditation is attained
By suspension of mental alertness
So only subtle impressions remain.
For others, whose desire is most ardent,
Clarity may best be achieved by faith
Bolstered by great energy, and focused
On singularly-pointed perception.
The intensity of the means employed
Provides further distinction in practice.

Meditation on the first vibration,
Which is the seed of all introspection,
Leads to disappearance of obstacles.
Lack of enthusiasm, laziness,
A wandering mind, instability,
Missing the point, lust, doubt, inertia,
Are all obstacles produced by the mind.
Pain, despair, nervousness, and disorder
Are coexistent with these obstacles.
For the prevention of the obstacles,
But one truth must be practiced constantly —
The mind becomes pure by cultivating
Friendships and bonds with those who are happy,
Compassion for those who are sorrowful,
Gladness and delight for the virtuous,
And naught but indifference towards vice.

Mental equanimity may also
Be gained by controlling energy's flow

Through measured inhales and exhales of breath,
Or steady application of the will,
Or focus on those free from compulsion,
Who are models of mental mastery,
Or the many forms of meditation,
Or by pondering on the perceptions
Gained in the world of sleep and sleepless dream.
This is how one may master all there is
From the particle to the infinite.

When the mind's agitations are controlled
It becomes like a transparent crystal
With the power of becoming all forms.
While the clouded mind confuses the word,
Its right meaning, and the knowledge of it,
The clear, pure mind sees only the object.
Subtle objects can then, too, be described:
That which is pure thought, and not physical.
The province of the subtle terminates
Ascending where pure matter has its end.
Reaching pure perception, the self has peace.
In that peace, understanding never fails,
And it is beyond the learning from books
Or that which is gained from sound inference,
So it supercedes other impressions.
Without seed, contemplation is attained.

Austerity, study of sacred texts,
And dedication of action to Truth
Constitute the discipline which will free
One from afflictions and agitations.
The five great afflictions are ignorance,
Egoism, attachment, aversion,

And the strong desire to cling to life.
Ignorance is the others' breeding place,
Whether they may be dormant, or worn thin,
Or partly overcome, or expanded.
Ignorance is taking non-eternal
For the eternal, Impure for the pure,
Evil for good, and non-self as the self.
Egoism is identifying
The power that knows with its instruments.
Attachment is the magnetism of
Pain, pushing one from such experience.
Flowing on its own in wise man and fool
Is the unending desire for life.

These patterns, when subtle, may be removed
Through the development of opposites.
Meditation destroys the active ones.
The remnants of the afflictions arise
As experiences in future births.
Our bondage to pain had this as its root.
From this root also grows the fruits of birth,
Of lifespan, and of all tasted in life.
Whether pleasure or pain is your fruit is
Based on the good and ill deeds you have done.
The grief not yet come may be avoided.
The cause of the avoidable is the
Absorption of the Seer in things seen.
The things seen have their manifestation,
Their action, and their inertia. They form
The basis of elements and senses.
The three properties are either defined
Or undefined; distinct or indistinct.

Pure consciousness sees through the mind, yet is
Identified as being only the mind.
The seen exists for the sake of the Seer.
Although Creation is discerned as not
Real for the one who has achieved the goal,
It is real in that creation remains
The common experience to others.
The attachment to things is the mirror
Wherein the Soul learns to know its own face.
The cause of attachment is ignorance.
The bringing of attachment to an end
By bringing the ignorance to an end
Is the great liberation of the Soul.
Continuous practice of discernment
Is the means to attain liberation.

Wisdom manifests in seven stages.
Sustained practice of the means of Yoga
Until impurity is worn away
Leads to ultimate illumination.
The eight means of Yoga are: self-restraints,
Fixed observances, practice of postures,
Control of life force, sensory restraint,
Concentration, Meditation, and last –
Realization. Self-restraint includes
Not injuring, not lying, not stealing,
Not being impure, and not coveting.
Self-restraint is the great obligation,
And not limited by race, place, or time.
The observances are these: purity,
Serenity, austerity, study,
And constant devotion to the divine.

At transgressions, the imagination's weight
Should direct the mind to the opposite.
The transgressions are: injury, falsehood,
Theft, incontinence, and envy; whether
Committed, caused, or assented to
Through your greed, wrath, or infatuation;
Whether faint, or middling, or excessive;
Bearing the fruit of ignorance and pain.
Therefore, cast the weight on the other side.

When someone is confirmed in non-violence
Hostility ceases in his presence.
When one is established in speaking truth,
All actions are subservient to him.
When one is perfected in non-stealing,
All treasures will present themselves to him.
When one is perfected in purity,
The reward is spiritual vigor.
When one has conquered his covetousness,
He awakes to the how and why of life.
Purity leads to body detachment;
Serenity leads to one-pointed thought;
Austerity leads to great happiness;
Study leads to what the disciple seeks;
And devotion to divine communion.

Correct postures are firm and without strain,
Gained by steady and temperate effort,
Setting the heart on the everlasting.
The fruit of correct postures is the strength
To withstand all the shocks of the body.
When this is gained, there follows the guidance
Of the life-current – energy control –

Of the incoming and outgoing breath.
The life-current is either outward or
Inward or balanced; regulated by
Place, time, count; it is prolonged and subtle.

The fourth degree – the sensory restraint
Transcends the external and internal
Thus is removed the light-covering veil.
Thus comes the mind's power to hold itself.
Concentration is disengaging from
Entanglement in all the outer things –
Thereupon follows perfect mastery.

Attention is a steadfastness of mind.
The holding of it is meditation.
Perceiving the object contemplated
Only, and not separateness or the mind,
This is true contemplation – Samadhi.
When these three – attention, meditation,
And contemplation – are in use at once,
There comes perfect meditation – oneness.
Mastering the meditative oneness
Grants illumination of perception.
This gift is distributed in degrees,
Is more interior than other means
That have been previously described,
But still exterior to soul vision
Free from the seed of mental processes.

One degree is developing control –
First is overcoming excitation,
Then the manifestation of control.
And after, the perceiving consciousness

Follows out from the moment of control.
Frequent repetition of this process
Makes the mind habituated to it.
And then, there arises an equable,
Constant flow of perceiving consciousness.
Steady conquest of the mind's tendency
To flit from one object to another
Is development of contemplation.
When, after this, the controlled manifold
Tendency and aroused attentiveness
Are equally parts of the consciousness,
This is the development of oneness.

In this state, it passes beyond changes
Of the inherent characteristics,
Properties, and modifications of
Object or sensory recognition.
Every object has characteristics
Which are already known, which are active,
And those which are not yet definable.
It is the succession of these changes
That is the cause of modification.

By becoming one with this three-fold change,
Knowledge of the past and future arises.
The sound of words, idea behind them,
And object the idea signifies
Are often taken as being one thing
And maybe mistaken for each other.
By becoming one with their distinctions,
Comes understanding of all languages.
Becoming one with bodily aspects,
The mind's activation of them rises.

Becoming one with the bodily form,
By suspending perceptibility
There arises invisibility.
Action is of two-kinds – dormant, fruitful.
Becoming one with both kinds of action,
There comes knowledge of the time of the end.
Becoming one with friendship and kindness,
The ability to grant joy rises.
Becoming one with any kind of strength
Like the elephant's, that same strength rises.
Becoming one with the awakened light
Brings knowledge of things subtle or concealed.
Becoming one with the Sun brings knowledge
Of the worlds and other spatial objects.
Becoming one with the Moon brings knowledge
Of the heavens and the lunar houses.
Becoming one with the Polestar brings us
Knowledge of orbits and motions of stars.
Becoming one with the navel brings us
Understanding of bodily powers.
Becoming one with the pit of the throat
Allows one to subdue hunger and thirst.
Becoming one with channels in the chest,
One acquires absolute steadiness.
Becoming one with the light in the head,
One has visions of perfected beings.
Becoming one with the heart brings knowledge
Of the mental entity – consciousness.
Intuition brings knowledge of all things.

The personal self seeks to feast on life
Through failure to perceive the distinction
Between physical and spiritual.

All experience exists for the sake
Of another – the spiritual man.
Becoming one with this experience
Brings true knowledge of one's divinity.
Enlightenment brings the intuition –
Spiritual sense-processing power –
Yet to the outward-turned mind these senses
Are obstacles to realization.
By weakening the causes of bondage,
Consciousness is transferred to the divine.
Becoming one with currents using breath,
One may levitate and walk on water.
Becoming one with maintenance of breath
And life-currents, one may radiate light.
Becoming one with the relation of
The ear to the ether brings true hearing.
Becoming one with the relation of
The body to the ether, and thinking
It as light, brings power to traverse space.
Becoming one with the unconfined mind
Wears away the veil that conceals the light.

Mastery of the elements comes by
Becoming one with their five forms: the gross,
The subtle, the essential character,
The attributes, and all that they produce.
From such mastery will come atomic
And other powers, and body perfections.
The bodily perfections are beauty,
Shapeliness, force, and the diamond's temper.
Mastery of the powers of action
And perception comes through becoming one
With their fivefold forms: their power to grasp,

Their distinctive nature, their inherence,
The aspect of self-consciousness in them,
And their purpose – the experiences.
From such mastery comes swiftness of mind,
The independence of one's perception
And mastery over basic matter.

The spiritual man disentangled
Attains omniscience and omnipotence.
By the absence of all self-indulgence,
Destroying the seeds of sorrow-bondage,
Pure spiritual being is attained.
One should overcome life's invitations
Lest attachment to things arise once more.
Becoming one with divisions of time
Brings wisdom which is born of discernment.
From that can one distinguish between things
Which are of like nature, not distinguished
By their type, character, or position.
This wisdom is star-like intuition –
It sees all things simultaneously.
When the vesture and the man are both pure,
Then there is perfect spiritual life.

Psychic powers may be inborn, or gained
By incantations, by drugs, by fervor,
Or by the insight of meditation.
Transformation into another state
Is by the flow of creative nature.
Creative nature is not moved to act
By an apparent, immediate cause,
But by the removal of obstacles.

Consciousness is built from the sense of self.
Consciousness, though one, is manifested
As the cause of many consciousness states.
Of these, the ones born of contemplation
Are free from the seed of future sorrow.
Impressions of unitive consciousness
Are neither good nor bad. Of the others,
They make for pleasure, pain, or a mixture.
From them develop the tendencies which
Bring about the fruition of actions.
Because of the magnetic qualities
Of the mental patterns and memory,
A relationship of cause and effect
Clings even though there may be a change of
Embodiment by one's type, space, and time.
The thoughts prompting sense of identity
Are beginningless due to desire –
The desire to live is eternal.
The tendencies are held together by
Cause and effect, by personal reward,
By desire, and by mental habits.
When these cease, the self-reproduction ends.

The difference between the past and future
Depends on the phase of their properties.
These properties, manifest or latent,
Are of the nature of three potencies.
Things assume reality because of
The unity maintained within changes.
The paths of material objects and
Of the states of consciousness are distinct
As is seen from the fact that the same thing
Produces different thoughts in different minds.

And if an object is known only to
A single mind, and that mind stopped thinking
Of that same object, would it then exist?
Objects are known or not known by the mind
Depending on whether or not the mind
Is tinged with the color of the object.
Mutations of awareness are known through
The changelessness of inner divine.

Because it can be known as an object,
The mind is not at all self-luminous,
Nor can it at the same time know itself
And still perceive things external to it.
If we think of the mind as being seen
By another more inward cognition
There would be an endless series of minds,
And a great confusion of memories.

Only when the consciousness takes the form
Of the spiritual intelligence.
By reflecting it, then the Self becomes
Conscious of its own true intelligence.
Taking on the color of the Seer
And of the things seen, the psychic nature
Leads to the perception of all objects.
The psychic nature, which is imprinted
By uncountable material things,
Exists now for the Spiritual Man.
For him who discerns between Mind and Self,
There comes the fruition of real being.
Thereafter, the whole personal being
Gravitates toward illumination.
Distractions arise from habitual

Patterns when practice is intermittent.
Removal of these is similar to
That of afflictions already described.
He who is wholly free from self reaches
The essence of all things that can be known,
Gathered together as a dharma cloud.
This is true spiritual consciousness.

From this comes freedom from cause and effect
And from the afflictions before mentioned.
When all veils are rent, all stains washed away,
The resulting infinite knowledge makes
The whole universe of senses seem small.
The sequence of change in the attributes
Comes to an end, fulfilling its function.
The series of transformations is split
Into moments, and when the same series
Is finished, time gives place to duration.
The pure spiritual life is, therefore,
The inverse resolution of nature's
Potencies, which have emptied themselves of
Their value for the Spiritual Man;
Or it is the return of the power
Of consciousness to its essential form.

Conclusion

It is possible, after reading through the preceding works, to construct a single ethical code that would satisfy the broader part of all five. At face value, this might suggest that a sense of ethics is ingrained in us, that it must be natural to be so consistent across cultures. Of course, that is not the case, otherwise such brilliant men would not have wasted their time expounding on it. Part of the reason for this impression is my choice in the selection of the works. For each word on ethics included here, many thousands of others exist. More important, though, is the gap between the ideal and the reality. We have had more than a thousand years to digest these ideas, but we can hardly claim that our societies show evidence of their practical application.

All five of the ancient writers realized that this would be the case. They only had to look at the history of humanity preceding their time to know they would be fighting their battle uphill. Looking at the circumstances which compelled them to take a stand on these ideas will give us insight into how we can properly deal with the array of ethics presented. Consolidating them into a single code of conduct, as it turns out, is neither desirable, nor what was intended.

Buddha and Confucius were relative contemporaries in the 6th century B.C., but faced very different kinds of societal issues. In Buddha's case, a rigid hereditary order was being established, and he rebelled against that order. For Confucius, the difficulty was a chaotic political situation and lack of guiding principles, and he sought to create order. The two of them ultimately came to similar conclusions – that society should be a meritocracy, and that a person's merit was determined by ethical behavior.

Buddha's struggle was akin to the one Christ would face six hundred years later. A priestly caste – the Brahmins – had consolidated authority beyond its right to claim it. The Brahmins were the arbiters of ethics in the society, and in telling people how they should live and interact with others, they emphasized the caste system as described in the *Laws of Manu*. That system's stifling of Indian culture and innovation would continue for millennia. Trapped by birth to be a prince and therefore part of the warrior caste, Buddha chose to create his own ethical system to counter the intentions of the Brahmins. The *Dhammapada* outlines an ethic based on knowledge and wisdom instead of birthright. It castigates the ignorant regardless of caste. The way a person shows merit under Buddha's way is through their behavior and their understanding. Buddha outlines what qualifies a person to be a true ascetic, a true monk, and a truly enlightened individual.

In Confucius' world, there was a fundamental lack of order due to the vast array of kingdoms vying for power in China, with the common people often caught between them. Power was accrued by force and wealth, and people often gained those two commodities through ruthless means. Confucius preferred merit as a basis for rule. While those who used force and wealth certainly succeeded in imposing their will, they did damage to the country in general and their hold was tenuous. Those surrounding themselves with able, ethical supporters, on the other hand, had eager, helpful citizens, so that the whole country succeeded together. The conflicts he faced and the solutions he found match our current world situation most closely, which is why I chose to put him first.

When considering how to use the ideas presented, it is important to recognize the particular struggles we face in everyday life, and our own shortcomings. In the end, that is precisely what all of the wise men did – they all spoke to the circumstances they faced. If we see wisdom in their words, it is because we face similar situations. When Christ rails against hypocrites among the keepers of the law – the scribes and the Pharisees – who can help but think of corrupt politicians, priests who commit heinous acts that have shamed the Catholic church, and televangelists who use God to make money? When Confucius challenges us to behave in a considerate manner, and to treat others as we would like to be treated, who doesn't think of a time when he or she failed to? When Buddha advises us to choose our friends carefully, most readers will immediately think of something crazy done in the company of ill-chosen companions.

We should mimic the road to wisdom taken by the wise, and not simply take their words as law, because while much of the landscape is similar, plenty has changed in the past two thousand years. To see that process of personal evolution in action, we need only turn to Marcus Aurelius. His meditations are of the form I would expect any consideration of ethics would take. He begins with recognizing what he has learned from others, and from the society around him. He identifies what is good and what is evil in his environment, and tries to establish how to deal with both. Despite the fact that he must have had incredible responsibilities and demands on his time, his process of reflection was clearly a daily one. Every day he would consider his actions and what he encountered. When he made mistakes, he reminded himself of the better course.

More than any other source, Christ is a visionary who presents ideal pictures – the pictures of what would be true in heaven. In the beatitudes, he points to those who should be valued and treated better than they are, and in the perfect realm of heaven will be. In the parables, the characters with the power to decide the situation always act righteously, even though real individuals in this world would have likely behaved differently. After the conclusion of most of the parables, Christ points out that heaven, or God, operates in this ideal way. By portraying what perfection looks like, he is certainly clear about his expectations. The problem is that, like most visionaries, he is descriptive rather than prescriptive. Unlike the other sources, he does not emphasize the need to meditate and reflect on actions. Rather, his only apparent prescription was faith in himself and in God (which is also one of many possibilities cited by Patanjali). The result has been attempts throughout history to justify all sorts of actions by faith rather than reason – not only in Christianity, but in all systems which rely on faith. So, while a Confucian, Buddhist, Stoic, or Yogi can explain why he prefers a certain mode of behavior based on reflection and experiences, a Believer cites only his faith in the word of God.

A close examination of the words of Christ, however, shows that he himself used reason and experiences to explain the behaviors he considered best. All of the parables are representative of this. It is likely that faith alone was never the intended prescription, but that it was interpreted in that fashion by the writers of the gospels. When reading all these texts, then, we should be careful not to simply have faith in the words or to follow them as law. It is very easy to see Confucius, Buddha, Marcus Aurelius, Christ, and Patanjali as great human beings who we are not fit to question, and whose words should therefore be taken as – forgive the cliché – gospel. The trick is to see them as fellow human beings who figured out a great deal by simply applying their mental faculties. Seeing them in that light, they are even more inspirational. Knowing that a certain level of self-mastery is achievable by anyone makes a great difference, challenging us to be better. Thinking that great men are born that way, or are gifted by God, robs us of that challenge.

The most perplexing document, from the point of view of the reader, was probably that of Patanjali. It really all depends on how you look at it. While I titled Patanjali "the Spiritual Man", I really think of him as "the Professor." The *Yoga Sutras* are very much in the style of lecture notes – the notes that a lecturer would build a course out of – and I think that is precisely what Patanjali meant them to be. This is Self-Improvement 101, where self-improvement is called Yoga. As you would expect from a course, there is a logical flow. It is very complete in its presentation of the key points. What we lack are the elaborations that would make each point clear. As a result, Patanjali is requires a great deal more thought from the reader, just as looking over your professor's notes would take a lot of effort to understand (if you had not already taken the class).

Instead of trying to satisfy all of the ethical precepts of Confucius, Buddha, Aurelius, Christ, and Patanjali simultaneously, we should use what they have said as guidelines for self-reflection. They are tools to be applied rather than laws to be followed. If we reflect on our day and how the words might apply to the stressful or problematic situations we face or have faced, that is far more constructive than trying to juggle a mountain of lofty expectations at once. Unless we train our minds to consider which choice would be the better way, we cannot expect to come up with the right answer in the middle of a tense situation. Chances are, in the heat of the moment, we are going to make mistakes. It is important not to be afraid of making mistakes, to recognize forthrightly when we have done so, and to resolve not to repeat the behavior in the future. Too often, the fear of error leads to a failure to appreciate when an error has occurred. When subsequently confronted with the error, people attempt to justify it

— especially in their own minds — thus ensuring that the mistake will be repeated.

The purpose of this book, then, is primarily to facilitate the process of reflection so that we do not have to repeat our errors endlessly. The key to an individual ethical code is not to have it all chiseled into stone, but to engage actively in the process of improvement. It is important not to get frustrated and disappointed by life, but to take everything difficult as an opportunity to learn. This underlies all ethics. Anyone who trumpets their own moral or ethical excellence has completely failed to grasp the basics. It is not given to us to know what challenges we may face, so it is always possible that our thought processes are not yet sufficient to cope, and that we may still have a lot to learn. To claim otherwise is, at the very least, to challenge the universe to come up with something really nasty.

In addition to providing us with ethical precepts, each of the five figures has a unique value based on their reasons for teaching. When the world seems chaotic, look to Confucius and his principle of reciprocity. If you feel stifled by an imposed order, look to Buddha and his middle way so that, when in opposition to order, you don't simply cater to your desires. For a model of how you should engage in ethical reflection, there really isn't one better than Marcus Aurelius. Some of us need a clear vision of the goal, and the rousing words of Christ are crafted to provide exactly that. Finally, you have the notes of an excellent self-improvement professor in Patanjali, and they are certainly worth meditating on since they require elaboration.

None of the authors wrote with a division between men and women in mind, even though the male pronoun was used in their words. I have not filtered out any distinctions of that sort — as far as I could tell, they simply were not there. It is possible that this is because they only faced male audiences, but I think there is good reason to believe they meant their words to be universal. After all, would Confucius have said that women should not adhere to reciprocity, be judged on merit, or fulfill their responsibilities with conscientiousness? Would Buddha have said that companionship with ignorant men was impossible, but with ignorant women was? Marcus Aurelius learned from the women in his life as well as the men, and the image of Roman women in history is just as Stoic as the image of men. The story of Christ and the adulteress, where he says "he that is without sin among you, let him first cast a stone at her," displays an equivalence between the faults of women and the faults of men. Patanjali certainly provided no alternative solution for the salvation of women other than Yoga, and it would be wrong to automatically ascribe the biases of his society to him when he made no distinction in his own work.

The way young people approach these texts will necessarily differ from the way their elders will, simply because they look on all of it with fresh eyes minimally conditioned by other inputs including socialization and experience. As a result, digesting these ideas will be easier for someone young, and more challenging for those of us who have been more thoroughly tossed by life's intellectual cross-currents. The older we are, the greater the burden we bear, because we have to deconstruct the way we have been conditioned – usually by influences we would not have chosen for ourselves – as part of our self-reflection process. It would be nice if we could simply look at our actions in terms of fundamental principles like the ones contained in this volume, but that is the gift of the young. Instead, we first have to understand the tacit assumptions we have learned to take for granted. These assumptions often block our ability to accept the course we know to be right.

The greatest example of this is society's emphasis on the acquisition of wealth as a measure of success. We are conditioned to accept this premise from very early in life, and it colors how we see everything. Carried too far, though, and we find that people who would readily embrace the words in this volume completely fail to act in an ethical manner in the pursuit of money. How is this contradiction possible? Because we are conditioned by society to expect it. We are told to assume that those with power and wealth will be out for their own gain without any regard for social responsibility or reciprocity. When financial institutions cheat people of their money or oil companies destroy the environment, their executives are baffled by people suggesting that they have done anything wrong. After all, they have merely fulfilled the goal that society taught them to aim for – the accumulation of wealth. That is the sole mandate of a corporation – it has no other purpose. In their private lives, executives are often genuinely decent human beings, and are often generous with their money once it has been gathered up. It is from this peculiarity that we get the phrase "it's nothing personal, it's just business."

Social conditioning is always particular to the individual and his or her environment. It encompasses assumptions regarding race, gender, sexuality, culture, class, religion, and all the other divisions we have manufactured between members of the human species. Ultimately, all of these ideas can stand in the way of us doing what we know to be right. And the longer a person has lived, the more likely it is that these ideas have become ingrained in the psyche. It is quite a challenge to eliminate the influence of such cancers.

There are times when the merits of one source will be more relevant to you than the others, and that is only natural. It would be wrong, though, to arbitrarily pick one to follow and to ignore the others completely. As has already been pointed out, life is full of the unexpected, so you never know when some nugget that seemed useless before might turn out to be the key. Nor are these five the only sources of ethics available. They were chosen because they were exceptional, but we look again to Marcus Aurelius and see that he learned from those around him. He learned a bit of ethical behavior from practically every person he met, and we should do the same.

The reason we learn from others is to avoid making the same mistakes others have made. It is not necessary for everyone to put their hand into a fire to know it will get burned. It is not necessary for you to make every behavioral mistake to learn it will cause pain. The texts in this book outline the broader types of mistakes to avoid. Speaking with others and thinking about the trials and triumphs they faced will serve to fill in some of the gaps, especially with regard to modern stressors. As long as a person is willing to meditate on his or her experiences at the end of the day, nothing more by way of study is necessary.

www.ingramcontent.com/pod-product-compliance
Lightning Source LLC
Chambersburg PA
CBHW051801040426
42446CB00007B/458